D0115390

STORYTELLING

The Indispensable Art of

Entrepreneurism

Rudy A. Mazzocchi

Award-winning Author
of *The EQUITY Thriller Series*

Twilight Times Books
Kingsport Tennessee

Storytelling: The Indispensable Art of Entrepreneurism

Paladin Timeless Books, an imprint of
Twilight Times Books
POB 3340
Kingsport TN 37664
http://twilighttimesbooks.com/

First Edition, December 2013

Library of Congress Control Number: 2013919790

ISBN: 978-1-60619-007-4

Book cover design by Ardy M. Scott

Printed in the United States of America.

To Dan Wigart—
A loyal friend, brother,
and fellow-entrepreneur
who took me under his wing
when I was so green behind the ears,
mentored me through the
'good, bad and ugly,'
always there to listen to my stories,
my Sherpa for the long journey.

Table of Contents

Foreword

The value of any new venture or sound new idea needs to be developed out of the nothingness of silence, ignorance and darkness. It ignites and illuminates the world only when the great storytelling entrepreneur lights the flame. *Storytelling: The Indispensable Art of Entrepreneurism* shows, with startling clarity and practical know-how, the process by which wealth and other things of exceptional value can emerge into the world literally out of nothing—nothing, that is, but the Art of Storytelling.

Storytelling takes you on a journey which reveals how the development, progressive modification and adaptation of your story is the golden thread and foundational core management practice which ties together all the others: building, focusing and motivating your management team, navigating through troubled times or excessive growth, maintaining positive momentum with investors and Boards of Directors and positioning the venture for a potential exit.

Everyone can benefit greatly from reading this book—whether or not you envision yourself as an entrepreneur. *Storytelling: The Indispensable Art of Entrepreneurism* applies universally to ventures of all types and is an essential, often missing, element in the fulfillment of any dream—dreams which depend upon capturing the interest and sustaining the highly-motivated commitment of others.

Award-winning author and entrepreneur, Rudy Mazzocchi, exposes his greatest secret of success and provides an enormous amount of "experience-based" illustrations and nuts-and-bolts practical advice. He reveals how to create and evolve the story of your new venture in a way that energizes and breathes life into what may have started out as just an idea.

One of the best ways you can be faithful to your dream is to learn and master the principles and practices by which successful storytelling operates. Without it, your dream may become nothing more than an insignificant billboard on a vacant lot. Learn what Mazzocchi reveals about the transformative power of STORYTELLING and gain a command of what is the single most critical set of skills to fulfilling virtually any dream, launching your business and manifesting your visions into reality.

— Michael Adamovich, Business Executive & Management Consultant

Acknowledgements

This may be the first and only non-fiction book I attempt to publish, given my recent affinity for writing medical thrillers, as mentioned at the end of my Biography in Chapter 20. Therefore, I need to acknowledge the contributions of many friends and colleagues who helped mold my entrepreneurial spirit along the way. Yes, they were all part of the proverbial *good, bad* and *ugly*, but as mentioned throughout the following chapters, this all contributes to the learning process making us better storytellers... better entrepreneurs. However, even though I'll intentionally leave little space to those disruptive hecklers I've fondly referred to individually as the *mad uncle in the basement*, rest assured they know who they are. It's probably wise to just leave those skeletons in the closet.

This book is dedicated to Dan Wigart, a special mentor of mine, who deserves a published autobiography of his own. Dan is one of those rare individuals, a kindred spirit, who saw something in me before I recognized any sort of spark in myself. He guided and directed me without a heavy hand, convinced me I had the right DNA without *telling* me, blocked and tackled for me when I felt weak, and stood by me when I was strong—an incredible human being to whom I am extremely grateful and blessed to have had in my life.

My career would have been nothing without the support of my executive colleagues and employees. They have been my most important audience, and when I expected or demanded loyalty, they unquestionably provided it... and it was an honor to give it in return. There are too many to list, but a few deserve to be mentioned here; Mike Renner, Tim Claude, Franck Gougeon, David Lee, Bruce Gingles, David Thompson, Frank Groenewegen, Raghu Raghavan, Jim Stice, John Kucharczyk, Matt Solar, Phil Smith, Tom Bridges, Ron Lahner, Ami Gupta, and Mike Calhoun. (*I know I'm forgetting several others... my apology.*)

I also wish to acknowledge those amazing venture investors who bought into my stories and worked with me to mitigate risks and build value. Regardless of the outcome, our collective intentions were always right, the objectives clear. Their continued input and direction, right or wrong, passive or aggressive, was well-intended and greatly appreciated. They've all made me smarter, sharper, honed my skills and fueled my perseverance along the way. In particular, special acknowledgement goes out to Pete McNerney, Dave Stassen, Rusty French, Kris Johnson, John Deedrick, Jim Bochnowski, Steve Waite, and David Milne.

And finally, I need to thank and recognize those who are forced to deal with the obsessiveness of this entrepreneur on a daily basis: my wife Gina, daughter Anna, son Luke, and stepsons, Jordan and Tyson. We've been blessed with a happy and healthy blended family who have provided me the strength and energy to do what I do every day. I'm an enormously lucky guy!

Introduction

NEARLY THIRTY YEARS OF DOING THIS AND MY LEG WAS still nervously vibrating like a jackhammer. I rolled the laser pointer in my fingers like some gambler would roll a poker chip, over and over in my fingers. While contemplating the two glasses in front of me, one with vodka, the other water—both brimming with ice—I rehearsed my opening comments in my head. A long draw on the vodka provided a warming sensation that calmed the jumpy leg. The second speaker was wrapping up his presentation. Within minutes I'd find myself at the podium!

It was a tough, intimate crowd of approximately thirty highly-specialized and wealthy surgeons with a sprinkling of spouses and administrative personnel. Due to the content of my presentation, I would be the third and final guest speaker that evening, sandwiched in between the cocktail reception and dinner—a "symposium" held each quarter at their exclusive country club. My audience was already fidgety, as the prior two stories had been cluttered, complex and confusing. The three of us—all early-stage CEOs—were there to solicit funding for our ventures from this wealthy group of physicians, but any sympathy I had for my two predecessors evaporated as I advanced my first slide. Immediately differentiating myself further, I stepped to one side of the podium and then took a single step towards the congregation before me.

My heart rate gradually returned to normal as I presented my enticing bait to this hungry audience. Key words would hook many of them, but I held back just enough to relieve the tension on the line. It was important not to come across as being too pushy—too slippery—like many of those faceless salespeople who littered their busy offices during the week. I had something special to provide... it was not only a revolutionary product, but also an invitation to embark upon a *journey* only a select few might be privileged to take with me... an exciting excursion that could provide them with something to supplement their current wealth.

Following my talk, there was a coronal discharge that filled the room, like the buzzing of electrical lines; many pushed aside their tempting desserts to join me near the massive fireplace in the adjacent room. They'd heard my story and understood its value; appreciated what was needed and asked if they could participate.

As I waited for the valet to bring my car around, I calculated the commitments I'd received during the past hour... at least $900,000. Over the next ten business days, that dinner presentation pulled in a total of $1.4 million—in the bank, with stock certificates issued and mailed out to *seven* new qualified investors!

To be an accomplished entrepreneur, you must be able to tell your story properly. The twisted road to success—*your* success—will be filled with enlightenment, dread, exuberance, fear, joy and desperation. Without exception, the journey will be long and any deviation from the path may well place you in danger. If it's of any comfort, when you do wander off that *yellow brick road*, you won't be alone, but the longer you stay there, the tougher it is to get back on track without starting over. This book is based on personal experiences and designed to provide you with certain "guardrails" to help you stay on that path... and to avoid those damn flying monkeys.

Remember the story of the Wizard of Oz by L. Frank Baum? How many times did Dorothy tell her story to others along her treacherous journey to the Emerald City? Her mission began when she explained herself to Glinda, the Good Witch of the North, after her house took out the Wicked Witch of the East. She refined her story when meeting the Munchkins, and it became stronger and more powerful each time she encountered a new companion—the Scarecrow, Tin Man and Cowardly Lion. Dorothy then put a different spin on things when telling her story to the Wicked Witch of the West. How many times did she have to explain herself to whomever would listen—convincing others to help or join her on the journey? By the time she reached her key objective, her story to the Wizard was fine-tuned, well-rehearsed and crystal clear. Not only did she achieve her goals and those that defined her journey, but others who believed and supported her story along the way were provided a handsome return for their efforts.

Dorothy was a storyteller supreme. The story-telling necessary to become a successful entrepreneur is not much different. In the beginning, along with the idea—the vision—the story we tell is all we really have... and yet it is the most important tool in our bag. If not told properly, we are doomed to constantly deal with evil flying monkeys and the possibility of utter failure.

CHAPTER 1

Definitions and Disclaimers

YOU MOST LIKELY ARE READING THIS BOOK BECAUSE YOU have a precious story of your own to tell. Many of us with creativity, drive and ambition will have something of supreme value we wish to promote. (Let me re-phrase that to read "something of supreme value we *must* promote, we are driven to promote.") Our audience could be small and well-defined, or massive as all mankind. Storytelling is very personal to me. I believe it to be the most important element of the true entrepreneur that represents our vision—our dreams. And the process we use to tell that story needs to encapsulate the faith we have in our belief and commitment. We owe it to ourselves and our audiences *not to screw it up!*

My cup runneth over with confidence from years of success and failures and everything in between. However, to better appreciate the perspectives and suggestions I'm presenting here, it's important to understand a few of my key definitions as they are used throughout this book. I have also included a brief disclaimer section below to address and repudiate any elements of my story you might believe to be *questionable*.

WHAT IS A TRUE ENTREPRENEUR?

This is probably one of the most over-used and misunderstood terms used in business. It's like calling someone a "loving-husband" or "workaholic." It means different things to nearly everyone I've discussed this topic with, and the majority of those who carry the title of entrepreneur have either christened themselves with it or had it assigned by those hoping to achieve such a title.

Merriam Webster defines an Entrepreneur as *one who organizes, manages and assumes risks of a business or enterprise.* That's basically it as far as a dictionary definition goes! In contrast, one of the Big Four accounting firms, Ernst & Young, has pioneered and continues to sponsor the prestigious Entrepreneur of the Year Award. Here is their definition: *the Entrepreneur is the creator of great ideas who strives to make them a reality.*

Since I've been fortunate enough to have been labeled an entrepreneur by a variety of different people, I'll take the liberty of expounding on my own definition as well. A true entrepreneur is not just a person with a vision, but someone who acts on that vision, regardless of the criticism, and despite the potential risk or loss of personal assets. A *true entrepreneur* <u>acts</u> on that vision to create something that may never have existed if such action were not to be taken.

An architect is not an entrepreneur unless he acts on his vision to build what he's designed, with his own money, sweat and perseverance. Likewise, an author is not an entrepreneur unless she acts on her vision to write that story, have it published, promoted and sold with her own money, sweat and perseverance. In addition, just as with the category of loving-husbands and workaholics, we can drill down deeper into a subset of such a definition of the true entrepreneur.

THE INVENTOR/FOUNDER ENTREPRENEUR

I believe this describes the ultimate entrepreneur. Remember the definition above? *A true entrepreneur is not just a person with a vision, but someone who acts on that vision, regardless of the criticism, despite the potential risk or loss of personal assets. A true entrepreneur acts on that vision to create something that didn't exist or wouldn't exist if they didn't take such action.*

The person who looks at a problem or shortcoming requiring a solution, whether a product or service, with the realization that there's not a current solution *for a reason*, overcomes conventional thought and identifies a solution through discovery—making it a viable reality. The Inventor/Founder Entrepreneur goes a step beyond, actually taking action to create a new solution, researching its novelty, and usually filing a patent application to protect it, in attempt to secure its value and control its commercial use. Here's the person who writes that first check, usually without asking the spouse, to file the application for patent protection. Unfortunately, this same person may not know how best to proceed. Although they are the one person in the world most passionate about the story, their understanding of the legal requirements for starting a new enterprise is most likely well beyond their realm of knowledge or expertise. So, in preparation for this new journey, those striving to become true entrepreneurs for the first time will need to learn some legalese, or at least be willing to shell out the money for a good corporate attorney. I've learned the hard way that the richer the story, the more important it is to have all the necessary legal protection.

THE START-UP ENTREPRENEUR

The start-up entrepreneur differs from our previous description in that he could be the inventor of the new product or service, but in many cases he is not. Start-up entrepreneurs are more business-oriented and have either partnered with the inventor or possibly "licensed" an existing patented idea for the purpose of building a business and commercializing the product. (From this point forward, I will use *product* or *service* inter-changeably throughout the remainder of this book.) These people will often times make the biggest of sacrifices early in the process; leaving or jeopardizing their existing "day job," working without a reliable salary and putting personal savings at risk. This is the true *hard core* entrepreneur.

THE PROFESSIONAL MANAGER

An individual hired by an organization to manage, fix or grow the business is often referred to as a *Professional Manager*. We can safely assume that "manage and grow" are intended to be used in harmony here. Why would any organization hire a professional manager to manage without the intent to grow? These individuals are provided a guaranteed salary, incentive package, health benefits, vacation pay, and the promise of continued employment as long as they perform as their job description indicates. Unfortunately, when some organizations survive and grow under challenging circumstances and/or rough economic conditions, this individual is often credited with being an *entrepreneur*. This is incorrect. This person falls way short of our definition above. I'll refer to the Professional Manager again throughout the book. The true entrepreneur relies on these Professional Managers to accomplish key objectives once the business is up and running.

As for the Professional Manager who is hired to "fix" an organization, this individual gets a *glimpse* of what entrepreneurism is all about, but still falls short of being what we've defined as a True

Entrepreneur. This is the "hired gun" — the person who comes in at the direction of the Shareholders and/or the Board of Directors to fix what is wrong. I agree that it takes an entrepreneurial spirit to turn-around a struggling company, but an old man with a youthful spirit doesn't make that old man *young*! So, too, a Professional Manager with an entrepreneurial spirit does not add up to being a True Entrepreneur. The Professional Manager is not deeply at personal risk if there is a failure.

WHAT IS THE *ART* OF ENTREPRENEURISM?

We all might agree that *Art* relates to creativity. By definition, it also implies something that one *practices*—such as the Art of Fly-fishing, or the Art of Medicine. Since it's just *practicing*, no one should really judge whether it's right or wrong, but people do take liberties to *criticize* how well we accomplish what we practice. Being judged as good or bad by any audience is a given.

While it is true that most forms of Art have a definitive beginning, they often have no ending. The Art of an artist evolves with time and practice. As with any practice, it's on-going, for as long as one strives to continue - changing, but not necessarily always improving. Such is the Art of Entrepreneurism — with one exception. The telling of the story needs to improve during the entrepreneurial journey or it will fall off the cliff into the abyss. Yes, the echoes of such an unimproved story might be heard again and again, but without any impact, without any value, without any credence.

It's critically important to realize that, just as we should recognize that one man's Art may be another man's trash, we should expect such a great distinction from most existing art forms when comparing them to the Art of Entrepreneurism. The "Entrepreneur's Art of Storytelling" has direct, visible and often immediate consequences that exist in the real world both of success and failure. Yes, we could probably also debate the definitions of *success* and *failure*, but my definitions have changed over time and most likely will not be equivalent to your definitions. Suffice to say, these consequences do not just *exist* in the mind of the entrepreneur... they exist in visible, concrete reality.

I've reached the conclusion that one cannot become an entrepreneur, in the truest sense, without experiencing a dose of failure first-hand. Actual failure, the threat—and even the fear of failure—can alter the way we deal with components of our story... and even to the way we present that story. The lesson here is to forbid failure or the possibility of failure from preventing your continuing the practice of *your* art. Cherish it, learn from it, and use it to become a better entrepreneur.

DISCLAIMER

Okay, here goes. Let's face it... by description, telling a story is usually perceived, by many, as just that... *telling a story.* Unless we're reiterating a factual event for whatever reason, telling a story involves events that have not happened yet, could have happened, should have happened, or may never happen. By the time my stories reach the point of actually being *true,* I'm usually on to telling another, now-enriched tale that is necessary to pull my listener into the next phase of a bigger story. Some may consider me, and many other entrepreneurs, as bullshit artists. I like to believe it's "storytelling" and an indispensable element of any successful entrepreneur. Unfortunately, many unfamiliar with the art will think it as proverbial *bullshit* nevertheless. Herein lies the true ART of Storytelling.

How do you spin a visionary tale of a new ad-*venture* that has not yet happened, but could, and should happen, yet has a high chance of never being realized? It's similar to trying to explain your dream or fantasies to a stranger—they are real, exciting and meaningful to you but difficult for others to appreciate. Even when you get your story across, why should they care? At some point it will most likely start to fall apart with *you* being the only one still believing your own story. How do you keep them at the campfire, sitting on edge, waiting for your next words? Why should they continue to listen? We'll explore this further in the bowels of future chapters.

Back to the disclaimer: I have no formal business training, therefore no M.B.A. (people seem to still be collecting those), and no one has given me the right to write such a book... but if I could be so bold... I'd like to think I've earned it. And now that you've purchased this book, I'm hopeful you'll learn more about the importance of storytelling in your entrepreneurial journey from my experiences, suggestions and annoying clichés. Many may seem obvious, but several of those points need to be restated and reinforced.

As you can read in my extensive biography at the end of this book, I prefer to be considered a "start-up C.E.O." I'm also a founder of companies, an inventor, angel investor, entrepreneur (see definition above), award-winning author of medical thrillers (fiction, fiction and more fiction), board director, advisor, consultant, father, son, third-husband, biker, rugby player, and... yes, perhaps at times... a bit of a *bullshit artist*. However, I hope by the time we finish this book together that you'll have a greater appreciation for my desire to be considered another great 'Storyteller.'

CHAPTER 2

Defining Yourself

Before we get into the Art of Storytelling, I think it's critical for you to think about who *you* really are in the context of becoming a practicing storyteller. You can look at the previous definitions, but more importantly, you need to consider *how* you want to position yourself as the storyteller, and *who* your audiences are going to be along the way. You see, as you proceed as an entrepreneur, not only will your story and audiences change, but so will you. Therefore, it's extremely important for you to think about who you are today, how your audience might perceive you (today), and how far you want to go. As one of my strongest Chief Operating Officers and close friend used to ask, "... what are you prepared to do?"

Remember, the art of being an entrepreneur requires continuous practice for the sake of improving—with the goal to succeed. Now, here's the first challenging part: you really need to be true to yourself. It doesn't matter if you have a background in the science of engineering, finance, or business administration. Perhaps you decided to drop out of the university after that first confusing semester. It doesn't matter. You need to set a series of goals that will eventually determine how far you might go before it becomes necessary to bring in that 'professional manager.' Most of us never make the journey from cradle-to-grave in the life of a company, so be prepared to do some soul searching along the way to see if you really have the fortitude or desire to lead a large organization at some point. It helps to formalize this early on in the process— for your own sanity, if nothing more. It's important to craft these personal issues into your overall story.

THE PETER PRINCIPLE

A Canadian researcher, Dr. Laurence J. Peter, popularized an observation in his book, *The Peter Principle* (1969), which describes the phenomenon within an organization of how people tend to eventually rise to their level of incompetence... they advance or are promoted beyond their level of ability.

It happens to nearly all of us. Think about it. We all have a defined set of experiences, abilities and desires, however large or small. We either get to the point where we no longer have the talent or qualifications to manage a growing enterprise, or simply don't have the desire. I like to believe the latter case reflects my persona. I've repeatedly taken a company from concept to commercialization, but seemed to have periodically hit the wall at a certain size. The business eventually no longer requires creative storytelling, and the thrill and challenge of proving the story true, no longer exists. The *pull to create something new* exceeds the *minutia of compla-cency* when managing the day-to-day operations of the business.

Throughout this book, I'll use stories from my own experiences to provide several examples. These stories are being offered to reflect the *good, bad* and the *ugly* of true entrepreneurism. Yes, there are people out there who may be extremely fortu-nate to have only experienced the *good* (i.e. success), but the majority—the vast majority—will not be able to avoid the experiences of the *bad* (i.e. failure). And if you stay at it long enough, you'll witness a bit of the *ugly* as well—a purgatory limbo where your venture hovers between life and death. You must be prepared for all three, and if you want to try your hand at this more than once, you need to be ready to tell your prior stories a different way, depending upon the outcome.

As reflected in my biography at the end of this book, I've been involved in over a dozen start-up ventures, usually as a founder or co-founder, and often as the start-up C.E.O. who's responsible for pulling the story together. I've experienced and survived the good, bad and ugly... but it's cost me dearly including two failed marriages, lost friend-ships, stress on my body and brain, missed years of seeing the growth of my children, and the sac-rifice of thousands of hours that could have pro-vided recreational pleasures. Making such choices to create new ventures that may benefit others at the sacrifice of your own domestic happiness, is not for everyone.

That said, I just started another new venture last year during my "spare time" while simultaneously serving as the C.E.O. of yet another internationally-based med-tech company, sitting on four other Boards, plus authoring and promoting two published medical thrillers. True entrepreneurs are wired differently... and are often times a glutton for punishment!

THE DECISION

There will come a time when entrepreneurs need to make an important decision. **If the venture is successful**, do you continue to grow and expand the enterprise? Stay with it until they remove you kicking and screaming? **If the venture is a failure**, do you regroup and try another new venture, now that you've experienced the adrenalin rush, independence and expanded wisdom from your mistakes? **If the venture is acquired** and you reap all the unimaginable rewards, do you pound your chest, absorb all the recognition and accept an offer to lead a larger organization now that everyone thinks you have the Midas touch? Or do you take your proceeds and go do it again? Every one of us will have a different answer at a different time in our lives, but regardless of the decision, you'll need to repackage and retell that story a different way based on the outcome. Build on it. Use it. Make it a part of who you are and how you tell your story.

THE NUGGET:

> *Be true to yourself. You're the only one who really knows what's right for your mind and soul, and the relationship you have with your family. Don't bend to external pressures to compromise who you really are. And don't fall victim to the Peter Principle... it will certainly lead to failure.*

CHAPTER 3

Storytelling 101

A S WE ALL KNOW, THERE ARE HUNDREDS OF BOOKS AVAIL-able regarding Entrepreneurism. There are even magazines and television shows about this subject... as if everyone can just step away from their careers and go be "an entrepreneur." Well, perhaps they can. Our country might be a better place for it but, then again, we'd have no followers to support all of us leaders, or builders to facilitate us designers.

I will therefore not attempt to give you my opinion about the ABCs of Entrepreneurism, but rather will focus on what I believe is the most critical single element of the Art of Entrepreneurism with a fundamental belief that *storytelling* has universal value, regardless of the scope of your ambitions. Think of the early Americans who founded and made this country great. They nearly all "went at risk" —pioneering, farming, industrializing, making, promoting and selling things. They enlisted the participation of others, creating something of supreme value with mere words. The telling of the story is an essential art, one that can measure and prove the efficacy of its excellence in the very practice of it, by how much the effect of its practice can transform a dream into reality, make great things happen, and generate wealth.

THE BEGINNING

I've often said that "it" begins with a *nudge*, which is more than just a spark. A *spark* of an idea, or the thought of something novel that might solve a problem or provide a new service, is just and only that... a formation of something from somewhere in your brain. It might stay there for quite some time, growing, morphing, or even stagnating at times. However, for the story to form, and the spark to ignite, it takes a *nudge*... the act of doing something about "it." This nudge might simply be your burning desire to put it down on paper or to tell a friend or spouse. The nudge might be your personal need to pursue your own solution because you're fed up with convention.

The moment you extract that spark deep within the recesses of your mind and put it into verbal or written form, it becomes the beginning of your story. Have you experienced that nudge yet? You'll know when it happens, and from what source. The first time you communicate your idea to one other human being, you've then started your journey as a Storyteller.

CONSTRUCTING YOUR STORY – PROVIDING THE HOOK

Your story is the bait, something of interest to offer your audience... to first capture their interest... then to lure them forward. There aren't many fish that can be caught without the proper bait, but just as with any good story (and worthy fish), you'll need a sharp *hook*... something that captures and holds the attention of your audience. Without it, you won't have an audience for your story and it merely dwindles back down to that spark... or worse... a smoldering ember. The hook is usually right in front of you. What made you want to create the solution in the first place? You were somehow made aware that something was wrong and needed improvement, so explain *why* it was wrong and *how* you plan to fix it!

Unfortunately, this hook has to be embedded within the proper bait. Again, not many fish are caught without the appropriate bait or lure. The bait is your story... the hook is what grabs them once they've taken the bait—bait being the content of your story and what it offers. The hook can only be set if your audience has an interest or perceives value in the solution to a problem that you've presented. This is your enticing bait.

For example; if you tell me that you've just developed a new chewable daily vitamin to improve the health of my prostate, I'm probably not all that interested. Maybe some other fish down the river might be, but not me. I'm already taking too many supplements. However, if you explain that your proprietary vitamin also will change the color of my urine from yellow (on a good day) to green, in the event my PSA levels are elevated due to the probability that I might have prostate cancer... I'm all ears... or as long as we're focused on the fishing analogy... I'm all gills, with an open mouth!

In the medical device business, where I've made my career, the most critical *hook* is to provide a solution to an unmet clinical need. My audiences are the Venture, Private or Corporate investors within the medical technology industry who will not go beyond my opening sentence without my presenting them with this *hook*. No matter how good my bait, reel, rod and line might be, there's no way I'm going to capture their interest... catch that fish... without hooking them first.

Once you have their attention, and they've taken the bait, now you need to set the hook before you can pull them in. Why should they continue to listen? What's in it for them? As with that fish that you have firmly hooked, you'll now begin the *fight*... that back and forth, give and take struggle as you reel them in. To prevent them from slipping away, you need to continue to hold their interest. You need to now determine what it's going to take to land them into your boat or onto that shoreline.

MAINTAINING THE FIGHT

This again requires you to properly understand your audience's interest as well as their motives for continuing to listen to your story, *and* at the end of the day, wanting to join you in playing a part in that story. Many may listen intently and enjoy your tale with great enthusiasm and empathy, but unless you have developed the right technique for keeping them on the hook, to hold them at the table, they'll simply thank you for your time and energy and move on to the next storyteller. How many fish have you properly hooked, but have gotten away? You will experience the same as an entrepreneur.

In order to minimize the number of lost fish, the best fishermen research the specific fish they intend to catch during their expedition. Different fish are attracted to slightly different baits, with different size or type of hooks. They may be hiding in different parts of the water and usually fight differently and require special handling to reel them in. Audiences (investors) are very similar.

In my world, when seeking venture capital, we will research the websites of every potential Fund that has been known to make an investment in the Life Sciences, and more specifically, in technologies regarding medical devices. Before determining which type of *hook* to use, we need to identify what kind of *fish* we're going after. Nearly all Venture Capital Funds have a listing of their managing partners that includes their bios, a summary of deals and possibly even a list of the portfolio companies where they might be directors. It's important to know that they don't have significant investments in other competitive technologies. It simply

means that they've already taken some other bait
and hook and most likely won't be too interested
to take yours. They're conflicted. They've invested
time and money already and your bait will most
likely be viewed as either inferior, or just another
fancier-looking fake lure.

However, be sure to consider casting that line to
those potential investors who seem to have been
previously hooked in the same part of the lake. This
indicates an interest, willingness and/or the expertise of playing in a particular industry. This is your
audience's—your investor's—comfort zone. They
like stories about these markets (this part of the lake)
and will most likely provide the necessary time to
hear your story. If nothing else, they will let you
know how others view this lake that they're swimming around in, and possibly make recommenda-
tions and even provide introductions to others.

"What's that? Sure... I'd love to give you
an example. The first thing that comes to
mind is my current company, the latest of
my favorite stories to tell. This company
is in the process of designing the world's
first electro-active, implantable, autofocusing lens to replace our aging cataract
lenses and to correct presbyopia, the loss
of near vision before the individual even
approaches the age to develop a cataract.

It functions very similar to the autofocusing lens on your camera, but is implanted inside your eye."

You see... right there, I summarized the core element of my story, the bait, and hopefully provided a hook for all of you who either have a relative who has had cataract surgery or will soon require it. Perhaps you're wearing reading glasses to read these written words right now.

"Too narrow or limited? Another good question... and very relevant. Yes, this is designed for a specific, rather modest-sized audience given the complexity of the technology, but the story evolves much further to not only 'hold' this very specialized audience, but expands to capture the imagination of many, many more. This technology includes a wireless communication link that allows us to send, receive and store data on the lens. With the blink of an eye, literally, we can eventually create a holographic heads-up display several feet in front of the user that will digitally present any data received and collected within their implantable lens.

I mean... think of it! We can eventually be reading our own critical physiological data with a mere blink of the eye: blood sugar levels, blood pressure, heart rate, and even daily calories burned. How about using your own implantable electronic lens to create a photocopy of anything you are seeing at a given moment that can wirelessly be sent to your laptop or iPhone? Or how about switching on that heads-up display to exhibit a GPS map or read that critical email or text of any kind? The system will eventually have the capacity to do so! Google Glass? No need... this is an implantable technology that could soon make any wearable device obsolete."

Here we see how the story has evolved not only to expand and hold the interest of the initial audience, but how it reached a broader audience whose members may not have been so focused, (no pun intended), on the medical or health applications, but who might find the expanded horizons irresistible.

However, given the need to find investors who were willing to invest in this very high risk, active implantable device that has never before been used in man, I needed to narrow down my audience and work on pulling the best possible fish into our boat. This initial audience included approximately forty-five Venture Capital and Private Equity Funds out of the thousands of U.S., European and Asian funds established to invest in development-stage ventures.

We then had to determine which of the remaining funds had an interest in the field of Ophthalmology ("the lake").

The next step in the process was to eliminate those who already had been hooked by what they perceived as a *competitor*. We ultimately found ourselves casting a line to only twelve squirmy, slippery fish. Although we landed a few, many broke the line or had to be released because they were too small (minded). The meaningful ones we were able to pull on board still required some work to keep them there. This ongoing process often appears to be never-ending.

THE NUGGET:

Proper storytelling requires some basic elements: understanding who your audience is, what they specifically might be interested in hearing, and determining the best way to "hook" and "fight" them through the process of reeling, giving them line, preventing them from getting snagged, and... in other words, keeping their interest sufficient to stimulate moving them forward to the next deeper phase of your story.

CHAPTER 4

Family & Friends

THE FIRST TIME YOU TELL YOUR STORY, YOU'LL MOST LIKELY get one of two responses: that it's either absolutely wonderful — *genius* — or totally ridiculous — *absurd.* You won't get much in between because you simply haven't perfected the story yet... although a caring spouse might provide you with an *"eh... really?"* You most likely haven't thought through all the details of the story and/or crafted the right elements to hook and hold your new audience.

And since you'll probably be practicing this storytelling for the very first time with someone you know very well, your initial audience will most likely be a member of the family or a close friend. Keep in mind, given normal relationships, they'll want to support and protect you. Therefore, their response will be to encourage you to either move your idea forward or to shut you down early to avoid failure and the *agony of defeat.*

There are also two things to be conscientious about here while verbalizing this first story to such an audience: 1) this will undoubtedly be the most incomplete, disorganized tale you'll tell during the evolution process of this story, and 2) you will most likely be asking this audience to be the first to "buy-in" to your idea. This *buy-in* doesn't only mean writing a personal check, but it also requires them to join you on your emotional, often stressful, sometimes life-altering journey! They usually really don't want to join you on this roller-coaster you're about to embark on, but loyalty and blood run deeper than any *hook* or *hold* that you will create for other participants. Ironically, your first such audience won't be all that interested in how you perfect the story as you progress. Their motive for participation will differ from that of your future audiences.

THE SPOUSE or SIGNIFICANT OTHER

Obviously, this is your toughest audience, your biggest critic... yet they'll probably stick with you through thick or thin. At first, you will sweep them up with your enthusiasm. They'll witness a renewed energy in you that they may not have seen for a long time. During this journey, they will see the best and worst of you as you hit the *peaks of inflated expectations* and the *troughs of disillusionment.* Some of these relationships will survive, many will fail. You'll need to stay disciplined and only update your story when asked, otherwise you'll drown them in too much detail, create too many expectations, and perhaps drag them along a journey they deep down really didn't want to be a part of all along. Tread cautiously.

OUR FRIENDS

Friends are friends because they share something in common with you; roommates, colleagues, neighbors, classmates, drinking-buddies, teammates. However, we often experience the loss of a friendship when they can no longer relate to us. We've moved on in a direction differing greatly from theirs. We've achieved an element of significance that they find insignificant, or created something that spurs jealousy or envy.

You'll find it easy to tell your friends your new story. It doesn't have to be too sophisticated or well-conceived. That's what good friends do—listen! However, if you're always telling your story and allow it to become too much about you and your damn dreams, you'll start to lose the connection with the things you had most in common. Because of this, I find that entrepreneurs have a difficult time "holding on" to good friends. So be cautious of how much, or how often, you tell that story to your close friends.

Many institutional investors are quick to tell the entrepreneur to solicit early funding from their family and friends. Again—just be careful. This often is done out of necessity, but as the entrepreneur navigates the peaks and valleys of his journey, strong relationships are important to mental and physical health. Even so it is possible to destroy key relationships from over-telling the story or forcing your intimate audience to listen. Such actions could possibly add to the daily pressures that will impact the health and survival of that relationship.

"Ah, yes... another example? Okay, an excellent one comes to mind that includes a friend and former colleague. I was in the process of fully understanding the concept of a new potential medical device company I'd been asked to pull together by a group of physicians from the University of Minnesota, along with their initial investors. They were in the early stages of developing the first surgical suite to include an MRI scanner in the same room—in order to perform brain surgery in the open bore of the magnet. The concept called for procedure-specific devices that could not only function safely within a strong magnetic field, but had to interface with the imaging capabilities of the MRI scanner.

While sketching out the concept in my own head, I received a call from a friend who was my former Chief Operating Officer at a company that we had just sold ('exited' is the more preferred term). We'd disbanded the senior management team, many of whom went on to other opportunities, but Mike was taking some time off, contemplating his next venture. He called to see what I had been planning and heard about my intentions to move the family and this new fledgling company to Florida. I agreed to visit him for an early cup of coffee out on the back deck of his house in St. Paul. As he placed the decanter between us, brimming with steaming hot coffee, I started in with the essence of my story.

"This could easily become the operating room of the future," I started, "… a surgical pit at the open-end of an MRI scanner where surgeons can operate on the brain while visualizing all the functional areas in *real time*. I watched as a surgeon removed a brain tumor from a patient lying slightly-sedated in the scanner. When finished, he did another scan that highlighted the small clusters of cancer cells, still clinging to the peripheral edge of where he'd extracted the large tumor mass. He then used a modified non-ferromagnetic instrument to pluck away the remnants of the cancer. The doc compared it to picking out large kernels of black pepper from his risotto, highlighted on the display just six inches above the open bore of the magnet."

Mike was an excellent example of that first audience. A friend, a willing listener, he fully understood that I had not yet perfected the story that was materializing in my head as I told it for the first time. As a knowledgeable listener, he then prodded me for more details while pouring my third cup of coffee. He questioned what specific devices would need to be designed, the status of the patents that was filed, the amount of capital required to reach key inflection points, and the regulatory approval process necessary to commercialize the final products. The answers were embryonic, still forming in my own mind, but Mike was already helping me expand the story.

Then there it was, rare and unexpected, "Hey, count me in... where are you setting up the Company?" I not only hooked and held him during the total consumption of that pot of coffee, but I got him to sign up for the journey; one that would become both mentally and physically challenging. Months later, he and his wife sold their Minnesota home and followed me down to Florida.

THE NUGGET:

> *Your story needs to evolve and mature as you and your audience do. Watch how they respond, listen to their comments and suggestions. Allow them to help you fine-tune your story.*

CHAPTER 5

Storyboard – the PowerPoint

THE NEXT STEP – OWNING YOUR STORY

We've now formulated our invention—our discovery—either on that scrap piece of paper, lab notebook or napkin. We've manipulated our solutions into words that form the story for ourselves, our spouses, friends and family. It's allowed us to convince ourselves that this could be *real*, that it's worth the time, energy, money, flesh, pain and tears to implement the idea. Now it's time to tell the rest of the world outside of our little safe cocoon.

Most good ideas and new ventures need to be protected or they could yield very little value for all the effort. The filing of a patent application is the first time our storytelling is forced to significantly evolve. This book is not designed to explain that challenging and rather expensive process, but reinforces the need to enrich your storytelling... to take things to the next level. However, before we reach out to others for what is needed to implement our new venture, we need to protect our idea. Filing for patent protection can be accomplished with our without the aid of a patent attorney.

During the most recent phases of my career, I found it most expeditious to file what is known as a

Provisional Application. This is a rough, but rather detailed summary of your idea, your story, in written form to be submitted to the U.S. Patent Office. It establishes a "date of invention" and preserves the scope of your idea for twelve months while you evaluate the market, perfect the concept and story, and further refine the details. Prior to the end of this one year period, you will need to formally convert your provisional tale into a patent application, now most likely with the aid of a patent attorney who is familiar with the art of your invention.

In drafting the initial Provisional Application, you can simply re-tell your story using words and images in as many slides as it might take, using Microsoft PowerPoint. Yes, you can actually submit the slides (either in their original PPT edition or converted into a PDF) directly to the U.S. Patent Office. Now, the best part of using this format is that you've already created the next valuable tool that is going to be necessary for your *storytelling*. Modifying your slides to include the following outline will be your rod and reel to pull in those investors, employees, and potential strategic partners. Here are the key elements:

THE INTRODUCTION

This tells your audience who you are and why you might be qualified to develop and implement this new idea or new venture. There's no need to overdo it here, but you'll need to quickly establish some level of credibility.

THE MARKET

Although most of your targeted audiences should have an appreciation for the market, they are most interested in how *you* view the world that so greatly needs your new solution or product. After all, your story needs to concisely tell how your solution or product is going to fit within the existing market, and how you're going to penetrate it and take market share. Do your homework. This part of your story needs to be both precise and as current as possible. It's important (and of value) to also cite your references.

THE COMPETITION

As with the markets, the more sophisticated audiences are going to already know quite a bit about the existing methods, devices, and players in this particular market. You'll need to convince them not only that your solution is superior, more cost-effective, and/or addresses a problem that no one's been able to solve, but you'll also need to provide them with a story as to how you intend to sell or market against the competition. Be sure to highlight the flaws and weaknesses of your competitors.

THE SOLUTION

Okay, this is the fun part... this is why you're telling the story. You've had a stroke of genius and came up with a novel solution to a problem, you've protected it, and are now showing your audience that you're prepared to focus on getting it developed and to the market. You not only need to show confidence, but you need to be well prepared and have anticipated as many of their questions as possible. *And* you'll need to show that you have the means to make your concept a reality. Provide them with a chart comparing the benefits and features of your solution to the gold-standard currently available on the market.

THE PROCESS

An idea is only an idea unless one acts upon it... most of us have heard that before... at least, most likely earlier in this book. Here your story needs to be tight and crisp as well. All the *creativity* was in your previous part of the story, now it's about the nuts and bolts. How do you plan to build your solution? Where? How much will it cost? What kind of team do you need to assemble in order to execute your plan? How much time? How will you launch and prove your solution? Yes, the *devil's in the details*, but tell your audience precisely what they need to know at this point as quickly as possible. *Process* tends to bore an audience, but it's critical to show them that you have given adequate thought to this part of your story.

THE NEEDS

Remember… you're telling your story for a specific reason to this audience. You're there to solicit their "buy-in," either for partnering (employees, vendors, manufacturers, or distributors), or purely for an investment—the capital needed to execute the plan. I've seen too many people present a great story and simply fail to tell their audience what they are seeking. You're not there to entertain them, you're telling the story in order to make them a part of it; physically, mentally, financially, or spiritually.

This part of your story *also* needs to be precise, but not pushy. Tell them what you want and need… even tell them again… but this is not the time to push to close. Don't even push for another meeting right away. Let the story sink in. *This* particular "ask" is to be delegated to your audience. Let them ask *you* for more information. Let them ask *you* for the next meeting. You've already told them your story. You've told them what you wanted. Just keep in mind that they won't say *yes* the first time they've heard it. Remember, you need only to hook and hold them. If you push too hard, you'll lose them. There's an appropriate time for you to *ask* them for something specific... but not at this point. Just show and tell again what your new venture needs to succeed.

THE CLOSE

I found it best not to craft a formal closing statement as part of your slide presentation. Make it personal. Show your commitment and passion for the story. Close down your laptop, step out from behind that podium, and look your audience in the eyes. This is where you once again bring validity to your story as well as yourself. Think of the stories you loved best when you were a child; the most comforting and memorable ones were those where everything came together at the end... *and they lived happily ever after.* Leave your audience with that same feeling.

THE NUGGET:
Before even telling your story for the first time, think it through, lay out the key components, structure it properly and then rehearse, rehearse, rehearse.

CHAPTER 6

Good Story – Bad Story

Yes, BEAUTY IS IN THE EYES OF THE BEHOLDER. YOU CAN have the best, most well-constructed story, but told to the wrong audience it becomes not only the wrong story, but a bad story as well. An inappropriate audience will most likely not relate to it, and therefore consider it "bad" before admitting they shouldn't have spent the time listening in the first place—another reason to ensure you know your audience before setting out to tell your tale.

As stated earlier, a good story needs to be told properly. If your story is complicated and requires an in-depth explanation for your audience to truly understand and appreciate it, *then take the time necessary to make it so!*

THE ELEVATOR SPEECH

We've all been trained to develop and practice that Elevator Speech—the time it takes to tell your story to a captured audience during that sixty-second elevator ride. If your story can't be told properly in this time period, then DON'T TELL IT! I've seen dozens of great ideas get turned away simply because the storyteller felt compelled to try and tell a complex story without adequate time. The audience will never fully comprehend the value in the story, and will not be compelled to sit down and hear it again. Their minds will have already been made up.

The popular television show, *Shark Tank*, is a perfect example of this. Here the wannabe entrepreneur has approximately two minutes to tell their entire story. This "elevator speech" approach sets the storyteller up for failure. How can someone possibly convey an entire story, provide the key elements, including the presentation of the enticing bait and the hook within, provide evidence of credibility and passion, signs of vision, determination and persistence, *as well as* the data, statistics and financial information that this audience really *needs* to make a decision to invest or not? If you are the presenter, two minutes gives you only enough time to present your story (the bait) to get them to bite, hoping you've inserted and set the right hooks. You then have limited remaining time (if any) to pursue the "fight" — which on the *Shark Tank* is the back and forth debate and negotiation between the entrepreneur and investors. It's nearly impossible for a credible investor to hear a two minute pitch, followed by a five minute discussion, to make a decision to invest time and money without serious due diligence. But hey, this is television!

However, there *are* lessons to be learned here. A good story needs, and deserves, to be told properly. Failure to do so makes a good story bad... very bad. As a result, the vast majority of the stories told on

Shark Tank never connect with their audience and do <u>not</u> get funded *on the show*. However, as revealed on many follow-up segments, several of them *do* move forward with proper funding and support once the storyteller has had proper time and material to present the story to a more appropriately identified audience.

"Yes, I can think of two or three real examples here... lessons learned the hard way. The most frustrating was a start-up that I struggled to get off the ground, a treatment for arthritic joint pain using a very novel 'mechanism of action.' My elevator speech was relatively simple, but the technology and related pathology of the clinical problem was extremely complex. Here's the initial introduction:
    'SynVEX—I like to create a name for technologies early on... providing one or two words that the audience can take away with them—is a targeted, non-pharmaceutical therapy for the treatment of arthritic joint pain... a procedure that can be done in the doctor's office, and applicable for any joint, regardless of size or location. It will be proven to replace steroid injections, oral meds and even surgery. We simply inject nanoparticles of ferrous oxide (tiny rust particles) into the inflamed joint... the

particles are rapidly phagocytized (or gob-
bled up by the inflamed tissue responsible
for the joint pain), and then exposed to an
external, targeted, pulsed magnetic field
(provided by a hand-held magnet the size
of a dental X-ray machine). The pulsing of
the magnetic field causes the particles to
heat to over 400 degrees Fahrenheit, causing ablation (killing) of the tissue responsible for the pain.'

The problem with this brief elevator
speech—besides not having enough time
to provide details of the stage of the development or the amount of capital being
raised—is that the audience is not given
enough physiological information to
fully understand the value of the technology. For example, it is not immediately or
widely known that our joints are encapsulated in a sheath of tissue (synovium) that
becomes highly sensitive to pain receptors
when inflamed... the actual source of the
joint pain. It may also not be known that
surgical removal of this tissue is one of the
therapies to treat such pain. In Europe, they
actually inject microscopic metal particles
that are tagged with a radioactive isotope
that kills the surrounding inflamed tissue;
(known as radiation synovectomy). Such a
therapy has never received FDA clearance

in the U.S. given the nature of an injectable radioactive material.

And finally, this short elevator speech does not provide enough explanation of how inflamed tissue physically engulfs small iron particles or how hysteretic heating can be induced by a pulsed magnetic field. You see, unless you're an engineer or part of the medical profession... I probably lost you right there as well!"

The technology summarized above continued to fall upon deaf ears and was eventually determined to carry too many unknowns to attract any serious funding. We were then forced to present this opportunity to many of the market leaders in the orthopedic industry, and *they* either viewed it as too risky for an early-stage venture or else too competitive with other surgical and/or drug therapies that they were currently marketing. Therefore, the storyboard, materials and related patents still reside within a file on my home computer... a forever beautiful story in the eyes of this beholder. However, as the wise Kenny Rogers once said (on multiple occasions), "You got to know when to hold 'em, know when to fold 'em, know when to walk away, and know when to run."

THE NUGGET:

Deflect the urge to provide that Elevator Speech before knowing more about your audience and having the proper time to set that hook in preparation for the tough fight to pull them on board.

CHAPTER 7

Writing, Reading and Arithmetic

Now that you've set the stage, you'll be asked for another critical piece of the *bigger* story... the Business Plan. Many armed with that M.B.A. may disagree with what I'm about to say, but I've found it to be true time and time again. The concept of a formal Business Plan has evolved over the past two decades. I'm not sure *what* they're teaching in business schools today, but you don't need to burden yourself with the crafting of a 150 page "Plan," as we were once forced to do back in the 80's. This Plan, which included a SWOT analysis—strengths, weaknesses, opportunities, and treats—has morphed into what is now known as a more detailed *Executive Summary*.

The Executive Summary is the written form of the story you just formulated for that PowerPoint presentation. Many will reverse this process by starting with the written Executive Summary and *then* extract the necessary bullet points for the slide deck presentation, but I'm a very visual person and find it more productive to start with the slides first, then convert them into the written form. Your choice!

This Executive Summary can range from five to six pages to—at the most—twenty pages. One VC investor told me it should be no longer than what he would have time to read while sitting in the men's room. The Exec Summary needs to capture all the key elements of your story, but provide more details and supportive information. Once again, this requires that you *do your homework.*

Follow the outline that you used in your presentation, but be sure to identify and read as much information as you can find regarding your market, the competition, trends, related M&A (merger and acquisition) activities, press releases from market leaders, and journal articles from within your industry. It's okay to "cut and paste" critical information supporting your story, but be sure to footnote where you found the references. This last point is important to maintain that credibility you've started to build. Reading all of this material also helps you build your vocabulary. Investors will be listening to ensure you "talk-the-talk."

Charts and images are critical. Your words are important, but make it (the Executive Summary) as easy as possible for your audience to digest. Don't make them work too hard to understand your value proposition. As touched upon earlier, one chart that identifies benefits and features over those of your competition could be worth more than all the pages and slides you've strived to fill. The same goes for images. Don't assume your audience knows what is necessary to fully understand your story. Its human nature for them to appear equally or more knowledgeable than you are! Some truly are... but many are bluffing. You'll need to provide photos or draw-ings to make your new concept appear *real*. Again, this is why I prefer to start with the PowerPoint pre-sentation. This is a visual presentation that requires images for impact. Use them here again in your Executive Summary.

STATISTICS and ARITHMETIC

Here's the reason why they call an Executive Summary a *summary*. We're doing away with that formal Business Plan because it's not necessary to include those twenty pages of projected finan-cials and cash flow analysis. These materials will be critical to your story, your business, and your financing, yes, but it's not necessary to include them in the initial storytelling. As potential inves-tors decide to move forward, they will ask for more detailed materials. You should anticipate this and have such materials ready and well-prepared... but don't drown your audience with too much material upfront. It's easier for them to assess components of your proposed new business one piece at a time. There will be many boxes for them to check along the way.

The Executive Summary is another important means to set that hook. It's that movie or book trailer—the synopsis of your story. Your audience will slip away if it's too long or not compelling enough. You will need to provide more details once you've hooked them... and there will be plenty of supportive material to provide: financial plans, a view of the patent landscape, biographies of your management team (as well as your own), cash-flow analysis, use of proceeds, quality assurance systems, and any applicable regulatory requirements and related strategies. For now, keep that Executive Summary tight.

I've become a "numbers guy" only because I had to! Remember in this initial story of yours, you are the Chief Cook and Bottle-washer, which translates to Inventor, Business-leader and Bookkeeper, so check and double check those statistics and then lay them out in a nice clean chart so you don't trip up yourself *or* your audience. Three charts should be sufficient in this Summary; one providing market data, another telling how your cash will be used to achieve critical milestones in your story, and perhaps a third showing how the ownership (equity) structure will look before and after you've raised the money required to complete your story.

THE NUGGET:

The written form of your story—either the Executive Summary or PowerPoint Presentation—becomes the outline of the supportive materials that you'll need to provide in order to move to the next phase of your storytelling.

CHAPTER 8

Putting It into Words

FOLLOW THAT YELLOW BRICK ROAD

What would Dorothy's journey have been like if she didn't have that yellow brick road to follow? You now have constructed the elements of a wonderful story, and even placed a nice white picket fence around it, to protect it from others who might want to make it their own. However, it's time to make that story flow as if you've been telling it all your life. The outline you've produced for that PowerPoint Presentation should become etched in your memory.

You know the saying, *"that's my story and I'm sticking to it?"* Well, until you have enough evidence to justify changing that story, you will need to strive to maintain consistency for as long as possible, with each and every audience member. Stories tend to fall apart when the audience hears them told in a slightly different way each time.

In telling my own stories, my most challenging moments are those when I get so entrenched in the story that I start to deviate off on some other tangents. This has often burned up precious time and diluted the key elements of my message. Therefore it's key to understand, before you start telling your story, how much *time* your audience has to listen.

Most stories are complex, and they deserve an appropriate amount of time to be told. In this case... don't rush it. Glossing over complex issues will only enhance the possibility of your losing your listeners or not providing enough details for them to fully appreciate the significance of your discovery.

It's also important not to start embellishing any points along the way... at least not yet. We'll discuss embellishment later on in the book, but this is not the time to be distracted with any fleeting thoughts of improvement... not now. Stick to your script! You've written it down, read it out loud to your spouse while he or she hid under the covers, and rehearsed it in your head dozens of times—hold to your delivery. Don't deviate. Don't head down some other road.

During the telling of the story, it's also very important to *read* your audience, but not overreact to their expressions or body language. A burst of enthusiasm from a listener can send you off on that tangent, just as much as closed eyelids can force you to re-think your delivery in midstride. Change the inflection of your voice, or stand up for emphasis, but don't deviate.

"Another question. Yes, you're right to ask... this deserves another real-life example. Very well, grab a tissue, because this might become a little emotional for some of you. It was my very first venture. I was young and still learning how to properly tell the story.

Our little company had a series of unique devices already developed and entering the commercialization phase. I had agreed to take on another major project to help deepen the story, to entice new investors, to build more value, and expand into other markets. It was a great fit. We had the proprietary materials and engineering know-how to pull it off. The device would eliminate an entire surgical procedure and provide benefits to the patient, physician, institution and even associated family members.

A congenital birth defect known as an Atrial Septal Defect ("ASD") is a hole in the septum, the thin muscular tissue that separates the upper chambers of the heart. This hole forms during the fetal development of the heart structure and causes the redirection of blood flow, thereby minimizing the amount of oxygenated blood that is circulated throughout the newborn's body. The lack of oxygen causes cyanosis, giving the skin a bluish color. Those afflicted are often referred to as 'Blue Babies.'

These newborns require special care and attention until they are old and strong enough to tolerate the required open-heart surgery to repair the defect. Sadly, these children live a compromised early childhood, restricted from running and over-exerting themselves, and are usually under-developed (mentally and physically) by time they are four or five years of age.

The surgical procedure requires the assistance of a heart-lung bypass machine while the child's chest and heart are filleted open. Once the defect is exposed, the surgeon stiches a small segment of polyester fabric over the hole which is eventually 'encapsulated' by a thin layer of natural tissue—the body's own defense mechanism to a foreign but biocompatible material. Our design was to create the same 'closure,' but to place the 'patch' using a trans-catheter technique while the patient was awake in a catheterization lab... imaging the beating heart with something known as trans-esophageal echocardiography, a probe advanced down the patient's throat.

Yes, the patient was slightly sedated but not under general anesthesia, which has its own inherent risks. No by-pass machine, no open-heart surgery... AND the procedure can be completed on the child at a much younger age. Now here's the hard storytelling lesson that I had learned.

I requested to tell this story to the Board of Directors, Senior Management, and the Advisors and Bankers of the large plastics company that had the biggest strategic investment in our young venture. My purpose was to ask for additional financing to carry us through the development and clinical stage of proving the technology.

My story was moving along nicely and I could easily tell that I had my audience well 'hooked.' The images in my slides successfully supported my story as I pointed to the hole between the right and left atrium. Upon using the phrase 'filleting open the heart' of a newborn baby, I heard a gasp from the audience. I didn't realize at the time, but it was from a father of a child who had recently undergone the procedure. Unfortunately, as a significant percentage of the patients did at that time, the child had died from a surgical complication.

Not knowing all the details, our eyes met and I started focusing on *him* while telling the rest of the story. He felt the connection and eventually spoke up, interrupting my flow, justifiably wishing to validate the concept of this new procedure. I then deviated… willingly stepping off that yellow brick road.

The room was sucked into the human element of the story as this father and I continued with an exchange of procedural information. All were hearing about the child's poor quality of life prior to the surgery, and the devastating impact on the family. Before I knew it, my time in front of this audience had elapsed and I was being thanked for the presentation. I hadn't finished the remaining ten slides outlining my requirements for capital or discussed how I would form a strategic co-development effort with the medical plastics division of the Company they all represented. Although my story was interesting and compelling, they suggested that I find the capital elsewhere."

THE NUGGET:
Stay on that yellow brick road!

CHAPTER 9

How Good is your Story?

I T'S NOT QUITE TRUE THAT YOUR STORY IS ONLY AS GOOD AS your content. Even if your content is just *okay*, or perhaps even questionable, your story can still be great! Sometimes it takes years of hard work to prove that the content of your story is valuable, or even the right approach at all. That doesn't mean your story can't weave a spectacular tale. In fact, the tougher it might be to prove your value proposition, the tighter and more gripping your story needs to be.

In raising that precious capital to move your new venture forward, oftentimes the term *good* simply means thorough and concise. Besides all those elements outlined in Chapter 5; Introduction, Market, Competition, Solution, Process, The Needs, and The Close, your story needs to include all of the components that you can anticipate to be on your audience's checklist. You see, whether they realize it or not, most audiences are box checkers. They're mentally checking off the key points as they're listening to your story. Often times these elements are related to their assessment of the risks... not necessarily that you've even addressed them all, but that you at least have provided an understanding of what they might be.

Not all boxes will be the same for each audience member. Some of them will be listening for items they've been trained to listen for, others are listening for key elements where they may have fallen short and been burned in prior ventures. A good story needs to anticipate and address as many as possible.

After telling dozens of stories and being in the audience for dozens more, I offer the following list of key elements that might make your good story even better:

- *Management.* Even though your credentials are strong and you're telling the story with passion and dedication, it is important to touch on how you plan to build your team. It's even better if you can show you've given this some serious thought. Identify the positions, potential candidates and when they might be recruited.

- *Use of Proceeds.* You'll surely need a chart or summary in your story describing how much capital you'll need to get to the various *inflection points* in your venture. Your overall story will have a greater impact if you can also show how capital-efficient your team and process will be! Give this some forethought and pick the right time and place to insert this in your tale. It's an important box investors want to check.

- *Inflection Points.* These may be obvious to you as the storyteller, but not necessarily visible to your audience. In an effort to make your story flow smoothly, these key elements may be glossed over. Be sure to emphasize specific points along the road where you believe you're building incremental value. They should be a collection of small and large objectives; e.g. the complete recruitment of your management team, first functional prototype, first production unit, first sale, or even that first time exhibiting at a tradeshow. These will become your key milestones when you and your team are eventually assessed for your progress against the initial plan.

- *Peter Principle Planning.* In the event you are unsure about your abilities to take your new venture all the way from concept to commercialization and eventually an "exit," then be sure to let them know that you understand your own strengths and weaknesses. If necessary, volunteer that you may need to recruit a new business leader at some inflection point in the future to take the business to the next level. Don't let your audience mull this over in their own heads. Be upfront about it and address it early on. Believe me... your candor will be appreciated.

- *The Exit.* Yes, I know... many of us are trained to *never* talk about the exit during our initial presentations. Everyone also knows it is dangerous to plan on building a company for the sole purpose of *selling* it some-day. However, I've found that this is an important element on the minds of all investors... how and when will they make a return on their invest-ment? Without appearing too eager or too focused on the *exit*, I recommend being prepared to tackle this ques-tion at the end of your story. You can even be somewhat subtle and show or speak about the recent exits of other similar ventures in your industry; i.e. acquisitions, mergers or even IPOs (initial public offerings).

THE NUGGET:

Construct your story to address as many antici-pated elements as you believe your special audience will be looking for... and then some!

CHAPTER 10

Go Tell It on the Mountain

ONCE AGAIN, LET'S ASSUME THAT YOU'VE PROTECTED YOUR story somehow either by copyright, provisional filing, method, design or utility patent application. It is now time to tell it to the appropriate audiences. It serves no purpose to "keep it quiet." To the contrary, you'll need to properly tell a version of that story for a variety of important reasons: i) to raise precious initial capital to fuel the idea, ii) to recruit a team of people who are qualified to help you commercialize your dream, iii) to maintain the support of your family and friends—through those peaks and troughs of your journey, and iv) to raise additional capital to build and nurture the idea. That last one was repeated on purpose.

There are plenty of forums out there that will provide you with a platform (and podium) to tell your story. In the beginning, no venue is too small. Given the opportunity, ask if you can tell your story at the local Rotary Club Meeting. These are great forums to help you fine-tune your storytelling abilities and to perhaps get over those public jitters. Rotary Clubs, Local Economic Development Committee Meetings, Regional Venture Conferences… they are all interested in hearing from local entrepreneurs who might someday lease some office space, hire local employees, or provide national recognition to their small community.

Take advantage of those opportunities, but don't get frustrated if nothing immediately comes from them. I've spoken at dozens of conferences, shaken the hands of hundreds of strangers, handed out thousands of business cards, and even kissed a few babies along the way... but the return on such dedicated efforts was few and far between. However, you never know who's sitting in that audience, or next to you during that late flight home. Many people need to hear the story several times before their interest is triggered. Many others may simply need to know that you have the staying power and persistence to stand up there and tell your story again. Many others may eventually experience a personal situation finally making your story "click" with them. And, if nothing else, every time you tell that story it gets easier, smoother and more convincing.

After you've climbed those barren hills a few times, and most likely generated some modest levels of interest, it's then time to make the investment in climbing the bigger mountains; the annual conventions. Every industry has them. Once you get on their mailing lists you'll be surprised how often you are asked to participate. Some are expensive; others may eventually reimburse your expenses as a guest speaker. Be selective, and be well prepared! The challenge with most of these larger conferences is that you'll have limited time to tell your story—sometimes as little as eight to ten minutes.

"Can I give an example? Yes, of course...
I remember those early years very well.
There's one in particular that stands out in
my mind. It was an invitation provided to
me by the landlord of temporary lab space
that I had rented to house myself, two engineers and Mike from Minnesota... with
whom I continued to share endless pots
of coffee. The landlord inherited the warehouse building from his deceased uncle
and gladly relocated from New Jersey
down to central Florida... part of his early-
retirement plan. While chewing on an
unlit cigar, his Bermuda shirt unbuttoned
to reveal fragments of an English muffin
suspended in the tight white curls of his
chest hair, he popped the question as if he
were asking me out on a date, '... so, you
wanna come out and tell your story at my
Rotary Club Meeting next Thursday?'

I didn't even know what a Rotary Club
was—thinking it must've had something
to do with rotary engines. After he further
explained that it was an informal gath-
ering of local business owners, I quickly
accepted, thinking it wouldn't hurt to start
expanding my local network. He then
asked if I'd be able to show a few slides

and explain more about my emerging new business. Absolutely!

Well, it was the most uncomfortable thing I've ever done up until that point. I didn't know the audience, who ranged from restaurant owners to managers of temporary employment agencies, didn't know the best angle to tell my story, and didn't know the venue—a small conference room at the local Sheraton Hotel.

Yes, there was a projector, but no screen or available wall to project onto! So I grabbed another glass of cheap red wine, waited for my introduction, stepped up to the podium, and just started telling the same story as I had told on that deck back in St. Paul, Minnesota. To my surprise, they were all fascinated... they'd never heard such a story. I definitely had them hooked, but of course had no reason to hold them.

When an elegantly-dressed elderly woman followed my presentation, telling a story about the grand-opening of her new jewelry store, the crowd quickly downed the rest of the free drinks and started to disband. Someone grabbed my arm. A silver-haired gentlemen who worked for a local bank pushed a wrinkled business card in my hand and asked, 'Have you ever presented at the Florida Venture Forum? I know someone on the selection committee and they'd be lucky to have you as a presenter.' Three months later I was standing before more than 300 potential investors, with three high-definition screens behind me, simultaneously displaying the engineering drawings of our first prototypes. The story flew crisply from my lips as I concentrated hard to stay on my yellow brick road."

After more than twenty years of telling stories in front of national and international audiences, sometimes as large as 1200 people, the scariest thing is being up there with a large digital clock staring up at you from a spot below the podium, watching it count down in anticipation of that microphone turning OFF once your time period expires. The key is going back to that original PowerPoint slide deck. Trim and cut, and cut again. Make sure you keep the *hook* and the *hold*... and leave them asking for more. And most importantly... stay on that yellow brick road!

THE NUGGET:

> *Hone your storytelling skills whenever possible on less critical audiences. Build your confidence, style and flow of the story until it becomes natural and comfortable.*

CHAPTER 11

Preaching to the Choir

A S PREVIOUSLY MENTIONED, YOUR STORYTELLING NEVER really ends—even if you decide, for whatever reason, to give up on the venture. If you do, you'll have surely learned something from the effort and will simply tell a different tale based on your experiences.

However, *success* will force you to continue telling the story to various different audiences at different times along the journey. Your audience will eventually be segmented into two groups; outsiders and insiders. Telling your story to those *outsiders* is similar to what's been described up to this point... and continued in later chapters. Telling your story to *insiders* is a very different challenge. These insiders are your employees, investors, bankers, lawyers, friends and family members. They've all heard it before. They know the little ins and outs of your story. They've been drinking the Kool-Aid for some time now. So what does it take to 'preach to the choir'?

DEDICATION

Your story will only continue to hold up if your internal audience hears, sees and feels your unwavering commitment. You can't run *hot* one day and *cold* the next, and you sure as hell can't decide one day that you don't like that story anymore. Failure is one thing, but giving up after you've convinced all those to participate in your journey, is something completely different.

CONSISTENCY

I will touch on something called "Moving the Goal Post" a little later... this is a subtlety that is sometimes necessary to maintain the overall story... to keep it alive, to stay in the game. However, consistency is extremely important if you want your internal team to all be pulling in the same direction to achieve those inflection points in the business. You can change major components of your story when telling it to new external audiences... most won't have anything to compare it to for accuracy, but being consistent with your employees and support staff is critical to ensuring stability and even loyalty.

ENTHUSIASM

As the storyteller—and story creator—you will have this innate enthusiasm and excitement to move things forward. As you build your team and start to increase their vested interest by providing equity and stock option grants to award their boldness in taking this journey with you, your enthusiasm needs to be the motivating force through difficult times and periods of disillusionment. It needs to be as inspiring as a sermon to a congregation. You need to light that fire in people's bellies and strive every day to keep it burning.

These three elements, Dedication, Consistency and Enthusiasm, are the foundation to building a *culture* within your new venture. Culture is not a storytelling component, but one that results *from* your story, how you tell it... and how you live it!

Preaching to your choir needs to come in smaller, well-timed, well-positioned stories. This audience has heard the overall story many times before, and may even have grown weary of hearing some of the elements they cannot either relate to or can do anything about. Therefore you need to break your story down into components that are relevant to your more focused internal audiences.

For example, telling the manufacturing process part of the story to your sales and marketing audience may not be meaningful to them... interesting, perhaps... but not meaningful or of great value. You'll need to abbreviate or tailor your story to your focused audience—with the realization that they've already heard the Odyssey version.

"Oh, yeah... I have a great example here for you as well. I was the interim-CEO of a med-tech company in Southern

Florida that had developed a revolutionary therapy to restore vision in patients who were blinded by stroke or traumatic brain injury. A portion of their brain—the visual cortex in the back, lower section of the brain—was damaged, resulting in one-half or two-thirds of vision loss depending upon the location of the trauma. The Company designed a photic neurostimulation therapy that forced the brain to rewire itself, stimulating adjacent tissues to provide the visual function that was lost in the damaged area. It's a physiological process known as *neuroplasticity*.

Although the Company had tremendous clinical and commercial success, we could not convince insurance companies or Medicare to reimburse the cost of the therapy, so patients were forced to pay for the procedure at their own expense. Unfortunately, many of these patients were elderly, living on fixed income, or veterans of the war, with little to no cash resources. The Company was in financial trouble, couldn't attract any more venture capital, and was forced to redesign a less costly technology and method of treating patients. The clock was ticking and morale was low. It appeared my story was lacking credibility and I was losing the 'hold' on my internal audience.

As the management team worked to 'correct the ship,' an opportunity presented itself allowing me to reinforce my story. One of our most successful patients was vacationing in Florida and wanted to visit the Company.

We filled the conference room with every employee, many standing along the peripheral edge of the room, seemingly steadying themselves in preparation for the inevitable announcement of more layoffs. I started my slide presentation without any verbal introduction. It was the clinical summary of my secret visitor — the before and after clinical images of her visual fields. They've all seen them before, the dense black areas covering three-fourths of the screen, revealing the blind area of sight... the small white boxes, identifying the limited area of compromised vision. Miraculously, the after pictures lit up the room with vast areas of whiteness, with speckles of blackness in the upper right hand corner—areas of residual blindness. It gave you goose-bumps every time.

I then stood, walked to the conference room door and pulled in the patient whose images were just displayed. Sitting her in my chair, I introduced her as she started to weep. 'Thank you, thank you all. You have no idea how you've given me my life back.'

She went on to tell the story of her stroke at a young age, one that left her legally blind, with only 23% remaining vision. She'd lost her driver's license, her job, and eventually her marriage. She and her four year old daughter moved in with her widowed mother and somehow managed to save enough money for the therapy. Six months later, nearly 80% of her vision was restored, she'd passed her driving test, and was back to working part-time.

There was not a dry eye in the room. This woman had re-told a component of my story which only she could tell. In less than thirty minutes, she'd instilled a new depth for our <u>dedication</u>, re-established <u>consistency</u> in my story, and renewed all of our <u>enthusiasm</u>."

THE NUGGET:

Always return to the basic, fundamental elements when preaching to the choir. Reinforce those enticing features of your bait that originally hooked them. Praise your audience for their courage to join you, thank them for their dedication, and share the tidbits of good news along the way.

CHAPTER 12

Embellishing

A S STATED IN THE DISCLAIMER FOUND IN THE FIRST CHAP-
ter, some may refer to this author as a *bull-shitter*.
I know of at least two ex-wives who would gladly
confirm such a categorization, but I only usually
default to such a practice after several cocktails
and when the subject turns to my athletic or sexual
prowess. But let's provide some additional definitions here before we start one of my favorite storytelling topics known as *embellishment*.

BULLSHIT

The Unabridged English Dictionary defines the
term *bullshit* (noun, verb, interjection) as "nonsense,
foolish talk, or exaggeration." There is also the
old American English definition of "eloquent and
insincere rhetoric." I would prefer to combine these
definitions and refer to *bullshit* as "eloquent exaggeration." I'm assuming the term *bullshitter* needs
no clarification, but just in case, *bullshitter* refers
to a person who delivers or expels such eloquent
exaggeration.

EXAGGERATION

Since it's now part of our preferred definition,
we need to shed some light on this term as well.

Using the same resources, *exaggeration* (noun, verb) is the act of overstating or misrepresenting the importance or truth of a subject matter. A start-up venture stating, *our new search engine technology is more sophisticated than either Google or Yahoo and we intend to own the market within the next two years,* is obviously exaggerating. There's no need to make such exuberant overstatements. Break it down and compare benefits and features, then show how you intend to take business away from the market leaders... truthfully and systematically.

EMBELLISHMENT

The term *embellishment* refers to the "fictitious addition to a factual statement." We embellish statements to improve them, add detail or ornaments, to beautify or make them more interesting. A melody is an embellishment to a song. When *photoshopping* a picture, you're embellishing an image.

Embellishment is critical to your storytelling. It should be engrained in your story and never excluded. However, if you refer back to the definitions of *bullshit* and *exaggeration,* you'll see there's a fine line of pushing this embellishment too far. The purpose of your story is to eventually convince other people to invest their hard-earned money, or to provoke them to leave the sanctity of a secure job to join your new venture, so you don't have the *right* to bullshit or exaggerate. If you abuse or exceed this right, then you've just jeopardized not only your probability of success, but you'll most likely damage your reputation and create a stimulus for possible litigation.

Often times, embellishment occurs naturally— out of pure exuberance or excitement while telling your story. That's the best type of embellishment. When it's pre-conceived or planned, it will appear contrived or a bit desperate. I've found that when your story warrants a bit of embellishment, it's best to simply tell your audience that you're about to expand beyond the core of your story. It then could be viewed as your additional *vision*, as to how far your new venture can go. Let them know you're already thinking beyond your current concept— that your story extends well into the future.

> "When do I dare embellish my stories? This is a tough one. I'm admittedly guilty of including embellishment in each one of my stories, primarily out of that exuberance mentioned above. When I'm fundraising and explaining the market opportunity, there's no immediate ability to exaggerate the size of the market, given all the available sources for statistics out there. Your audience will either know you're bullshitting, or quickly know shortly after they finish their homework, here known as *due diligence*. However, I have been known to push the vision of where the technology

might go. Remember that implantable autofocusing lens mentioned in Chapter 3?

After reviewing the technology behind Google Glass, which provides the opportunity for the wearer to project a navigational map onto the system's 'heads-up display,' we explored the possibility of providing such a feature from with inside the eye. The implantable microchips and optical components surely had the capacity, and the wireless RF communication coils could possibly receive and send the appropriate data, but the challenge was with the onboard power cells. They needed to provide nearly three times the energy capacity. Surely, with the evolution of implantable battery technology, such a future generation product could be possible... wouldn't you agree? Well, okay, the lens also needs to be pixelated properly, but those engineers back in the lab could figure that out, too!

So off I went, spinning the end of my tale, showing images that started with Lee Majors as the Six Million Dollar Man, linking them to the glowing-red eyes of Arnold as The Terminator, and finally to the display of information on the masked lens of Iron Man. Imagine all the commercial applications of such a technology beyond the treatment of cataracts!

Well, of course! There are often a few rolling eyes in the audience, but the ear-to-ear grins were worth the time of embellishment. However, as a seasoned story-teller, I was quick to add that these were future designs, requiring additional development efforts... and a helluva lot more capital."

"Has it ever back-fired on me? In reflecting back on my experiences, perhaps I should also follow with a word of caution: *it's still important to know your audience before weaving an embellishing web.* On one occasion, I was asked to meet a major investor who also sat on my Board of Directors. He sounded very stern, and asked... no, he actually *demanded...* that I immediately fly up to Minneapolis to have breakfast with him that following Monday morning in early December. He was a well-known Venture Capitalist whose special request, I couldn't take lightly.

Four days later, while hovering over yet another steaming black cup of coffee, he sat before me without even removing his coat and scarf.

'I've been reviewing the materials from our last Board call more closely, to prepare for an upcoming meeting with the investors of our Fund.' He finally took off his gloves, but still didn't even look at the menu. My mind immediately wondered to the metaphor of *the gloves coming off.*

He continued, '...and this is the third time that you and your management team have missed your revenue projections. This is not acceptable, and sooner or later *you* are going to be held accountable for this.'

I wasn't well prepared for such a confrontation, and wished I'd flushed out the topics of the meeting prior to booking the flight... to at least been able to provide an explanatory story. Unfortunately, all I could do was go on the defense.

'We've been keeping the Board updated each quarter and have altered our sales projections according to the delays in FDA approvals and physician training sessions. You know very well that these plans have been built from the bottom up using dozens of critical assumptions that could—'

'Don't bullshit me,' he barked back. 'I'm talking about the initial revenue projections that you pitched to me prior to our investment. You've constantly been moving the goal posts with every little glitch that occurs.'

As I clenched my coffee cup in unison to the clenching of my jaw, I suddenly realized I didn't truly understand this audience member as well as I thought I did. I should have learned more about his investment strategy and history before providing him with the same story I told the other venture investors. He was obviously under some pressure from *his* investors who simply equated top-line growth with value creation. He followed with another confirming statement before I was able to respond.

Leaning closer, he glared into my eyes, 'this kind of misrepresentation, my friend, is what stimulates law suits.'

I fought the urge to tell him that he shouldn't use the term *friend* and *law suit* in the same sentence. Instead, I went on to explain once again that the sales projections used in our initial plan were done well in advance of even having a final product with definitive benefits and features that would drive a sales and marketing strategy. He knew that... I knew he knew that, and he knew that I knew that he knew it. After an hour of discussion, we were finally back on the same page, but to this day the concept of *moving the goal posts* is anticipated in each and every one of my storytelling processes. As all entrepreneurs come to understand, it's often essential to move the goal posts sometimes to simply stay in the game. This was an example of neither exaggerating nor embellishing, but to this particular audience member, it was an exaggerated embellishment that was nearly fraudulent."

This represents another justification for the engagement of a corporate attorney when piecing together the written components of your story. Just as I feebly attempted to provide a disclaimer at the beginning of this book, you will need the appropriate disclaimer language in any sort of Offering Memorandum that you might circulate to potential investors. There's no such thing as a free "get out of jail card," but good corporate counsel can save you a great deal of long-term anguish and potential liabilities.

THE NUGGET:

Never bullshit or exaggerate. It's okay to pepper your story with a bit of embellishment, but do so with caution... and only after you have your audience hooked with the basic facts. It also is worth the time and costs to have professional legal review of any formal documents that you plan to put out on the street.

CHAPTER 13

Editing your Story

IN A PREVIOUS CHAPTER, THE FOLLOWING STATEMENT WAS made: *Well, until you have enough evidence to justify changing that story, you will need to strive to maintain consistency for as long as possible, with each and every audience member. Stories tend to fall apart when the audience hears it told slightly different each time.*

This holds to be true. However, there are four reasons for when you should consider revising your story; i) to integrate those thoughtful comments and feedback from your audience, ii) when you've made actual changes, progress or encountered delays with your development—even though some people might view this as moving the goal post, iii) to refresh and update your storytelling to hold onto audiences that tend to have a short attention span, and iv) to reinvent the mission and goals of the company—which is the topic entirely dedicated to the next chapter.

It wasn't until my third venture did I appreciate the importance of tracking the changes in your story. Looking back through my electronic files, prior revisions of Executive Summaries and PPT Presentations are now nicely numbered and filed chronologically. There are dozens of folders that are segregated by the type of audience: venture investor, private investors, corporate investors, and even 'staff meetings.' Each story edited slightly to meet the particular interest of a specific audience. One file contains forty-seven different versions of a PowerPoint presentation.

Why forty-seven?

The first dozen slide presentations were designed to tell my story from beginning to end within twenty minutes. Enough time to capture my audience's interest, but not deep enough for a serious investor who eventually provides me with sixty to ninety minutes—an hour long examination to determine whether or not I really thought it all the way through. Therefore many of them paint the same picture; the later ones simply have more definition and color.

The next series of actual revisions provide answers to those new audience questions that were not initially anticipated. It took me a while to figure out who really wanted to hear my personal thoughts on the 'exit' — the act of selling your company for a handsome return—and which audience members might view this as a *distraction* and improper element of the story to be focused on at this time. This difficult topic changes with the type of investor, stage of the company, and even the climate and conditions of our economy when the story is being told. I've even had to change the timing and ending of my story after learning that certain venture capital investors had altered *their* 'investment strategy' — needing to have visibility to an 'exit' within three years of making their investment. I therefore built the ending of my story to show that the objective to sell the company in that time period *could* be met. Obviously, there was no way I could, or would, promise any specific valuation or return on their investment.

There are then those revisions needing to be made because of unexpected changes in your development plan. Usually this is a bad thing. There's always something that creates a delay; a redesign, production glitch, or even something out of your control such as a backorder from a vendor. Seldom does luck intervene and manage to shorten the timeline or provide a shortcut to 'come under budget.' Yes, some folks will view these revisions as 'moving the goal-posts'! When you make these revisions for this purpose, it's important to inform every one of your audience members, as soon as possible. Telling some, and not the others, will cause great confusion down the road... telling no one, will spurn great distrust and lack of confidence in you and your team.

The final reason to periodically revise your story is the most rewarding... and enjoyable. When things are trending well, and you finally have time to step back, take a breath and assess the fruits of your labor, now is the time to refresh that story. Make it look, feel and sound new. Perhaps change your logo. *The average American company changes its*

*logo from seven to twelve times during the course of its
lifetime. Pepsi Cola is on its eleventh logo design!*

Even changing the font and colors on your presentation will renew your story. My favorite revisions are done by re-ordering the components of your story. Let me give you a brief example of another interesting story that I was telling several years ago. A story about a company called SOLARIBUS.

"The company has licensed and redesigned a technology that had been used for military applications during the Vietnam War. Helicopters would fly over the thick canopies of the jungle, and with the aid of a hyper-spectral, infra-red camera suspended from the belly of the chopper, they would be able to locate the hiding enemy soldiers below. They then advanced the technology and developed an algorithm that would eventually reveal whether the soldier was an American or a Vietnamese, by simply assessing the skin chemistry. This technology was also later used by pilots flying over orange groves in Florida to determine which trees might be infected with a specific disease. The leaves of the tree would exhibit a different spectral color if it was infected by citrus canker long before the disease was detectable by any other means.

SOLARIBUS has redesigned this hyper-spectral imaging technology to provide the dermatologist a body scanner that could image an entire patient to detect any early signs of skin cancer deep within the dermal layers before it was even visible on the skin's surface by the naked eye. This technology could pre-diagnose life-threatening melanomas even before it was necessary to perform a physical biopsy of a skin lesion. Early detection could eliminate all skin cancers!"

So that was the original story I enjoyed telling. I'd sprinkle in pictures of silhouettes of soldiers, trained in guerilla warfare, hiding in the thick bush, as well as aerial views of acres of orange trees with specks of neon yellow revealing those unfortunate arbors infected with canker. Now here's a later version... same story... just reordered a bit to freshen it up!

"SOLARIBUS is developing a novel technology using hyper-spectral imaging to detect early signs of skin cancer. The World Health Organization has determined that mortalities caused by skin cancers, such as melanoma, can be completely eliminated if the afflicted cells can be detected early enough. The Company has prototyped a body scanner that can be used in the dermatologist's office that would identify the precursor of cancerous cells below the surface of the skin long before it is ever detectable by the naked eye. Early detection equals Cure!

This proven technology has been used by hyper-spectral scanners suspended beneath surveillance helicopters to differentiate between American and North Vietnamese soldiers hiding in the juggles of Vietnam. It is also currently in use to detect citrus canker in the leaves of diseased citrus trees in Florida, long before they can be assessed by any other means. This is where I'd show a slide of those soldiers and diseased citrus trees from 10,000 feet, along-side a spectral image of a cancer lesion beneath the skin."

This second version presents the bait within the opening sentence then goes on to explain and validate the technology, setting that hook nice and deep. The first version leads with an interesting story about the technology but may leave the audience wondering 'where's the bait that should be grabbing my interest?' Is this a story about a military technology for homeland security or about how it might be used to improve the yield of citrus crops in Florida? No, it's a potential cure for skin cancer!

THE NUGGET:

When editing or revising your story, only edit with a purpose. Think it through and make sure your story maintains the continuity of your previously told stories for the purpose of achieving specific objectives.

CHAPTER 14

Reinventing your Story

I KNOW... *REINVENTING MYSELF, REINVENTING MY COM-pany...* it all sounds like another overused business cliché. However, if you stick with your story long enough, your business will be in one of three places; 1) barely surviving, 2) stalled, or 3) successful and running out of room to grow. It's now time to reinvent your story and exit that tortuous yellow brick road and deliberately merge onto another redesigned path.

SURVIVAL

You've done everything feasibly possible to stay on the yellow brick road, spun the best of tales to multiple audiences, many of whom have joined you for the journey. You've fought off those witches, mad uncles in the basement and damn flying monkeys, but it's only been sufficient to survive. You've now exhausted all sources for new audiences. The old fishing hole is all fished out. It's time for a new story to help pull you out of the trenches.

Reinventing the company, regardless of the reason, requires new investors... new capital. It's not as easy as simply going back to the beginning and starting over with a new fresh story. This new story has to take into account why you chose your original path and why it failed. There's also those valuable employees. They've believed in your initial story, made commitments, and became important components to your story. You now need to test the merits of your *new* story on this very challenging audience. You can't bluff your way through it... there's nowhere to hide.

Failure is more painful if you don't have the courage to admit when it occurs. Attempting to get back on the correct path is admirable (and worth the effort), but hanging on to a story you know will not have a happy ending is reckless. Your employees and key audience members will maintain their respect for you, and most likely sign-up for your new journey, if you have the courage to set a new direction. You'll probably only have one chance and you'll have to move quickly, but make sure you do the same amount of upfront work... perhaps even a bit more wisely this time around.

STALLED

The need to reinvent your story may occur in the midst of moderate success. Everything feels like it's moving in the right direction, according to plan, until there's a loss in momentum... a stall. This is a dangerous place because many entrepreneurs don't see it coming. The loss of momentum of a business shadows an underlying problem that creeps up on an organization. It may be the delay—or complete failure—to execute on a new product launch, or perhaps just the opposite... your team is so excited about a new expansion that they take their eyes off of the core business. A stall may even occur if you fail to anticipate the approach of the top of your company's growth curve.

This is where your advanced audiences, such as the Board of Directors, should be of value. It also may be very wise to expand your advanced audiences to include an Advisory Board or external Marketing Committee with a different perspective on the ramping of your business. Test your revised story with them first. Seek their guidance and support to help pull you out of the stall. Adjust... redefine your story and push through those speedbumps on that yellow brick road.

TOPPED OUT

Okay, hold on tight. This is where many of us learn the hard facts of the Peter Principle. You'll need to dig deep if you want to survive what might be perceived as the top end of your growth trajectory. Many Boards will start to discuss a succession plan... to bring in a professional manager who might overhaul the product or service, modify the infrastructure (management and processes), or perhaps drive an aggressive merger and acquisition plan. Here you might need to reinvent both yourself *and* your company. Remember your roots as an entrepreneur... identify a catalyst that can influence a new direction or growth plan. Innovate! Drive new technology development, improve product branding, and strive to stimulate a new culture in your business. And don't forget... focus on the new story that includes fresh bait and a bigger hook.

THE NUGGET:

Reinventing your company requires a bold new story. It's often beneficial to commit to reinventing the company before there's even a recognizable need. It doesn't come naturally and takes a great deal of courage.

CHAPTER 15

When to Let Go

IREALIZE THIS IS STARTING TO SOUND REDUNDANT, BUT THIS refers to a different type of "sticking to it-ism." The previous emphasis on sticking to your story related to the actual *telling* of the story—the importance of maintaining the key elements of your story that shows consistency and garners credibility. Now let's discuss your ability to *continue* telling your story... no matter *what*... never letting go!

Face it, at some point telling the same story over and over again becomes tedious. And if you don't tell it with that same level of compassion and energy every time, you might as well not tell it at all.

We also know that *failure* is part of being an entrepreneur. None of us are going to knock that ball out of the park every time we take a swing. We're going to either win or lose the game, but the key is to score as often as possible, play with heart, and win or lose with grace and dignity.

I believe it was Winston Churchill who coined the old adage, *"never, never, never give up,"* but here we need to realize that there's a big difference in "giving up" and knowing when to simply "play out the game." None of us would strike out in the first inning, flip the bird to our fans and team- mates, and quit the game, would we? There are subtle differences in giving up and playing out the game—regardless of the disappointment of failed performance.

GIVING UP

I hope you take my word for it that I'm not bullshitting when I tell ya that I've never really given up on anything… even those two prior failed marriages of mine. I'm also not saying that it's a good thing either. Playing something out to the end that you know isn't going to end well, is *not* necessarily healthy or productive. (This is especially true if you're gambling with someone else's money.) Failed marriages in which the individuals seek counseling, fight and yell in hopes of finding common ground, and even try a 'trial separation,' are at least those attempting to *play out the game.* However, if you've ever been the one who simply packed up their bags and walked out the door with no discussion or attempt to come up with another game-plan, then you can join the ranks of those who have simply *given up.*

"Now, that's another good question… there *is* something in between! I'm not sure I can provide an analogy in marriage, but I can think of one example in a prior business.

We had actually turned the corner with the development of a technology that could be described as a disposable GPS system designed for the brain surgeon. It was mounted to the patient's skull and replaced a very outdated and barbaric means by which to secure the patient's head to the surgical table to perform a brain biopsy. The conventional technology bolted the patient to this 'headframe' with four screws into the skull. Attached to this headframe was something that looked like a rotatable compass and protractor. Our small company had just received FDA approval and we were ramping up production to supply anticipated needs of the market. My Board also instructed me to go out and find the most knowledgeable and respected Vice President of Sales & Marketing who could drive the business 'through the roof.'

So, with a more complete story to tell, I went out and recruited the best senior person our limited funds could buy. To protect the innocent, let's kindly refer him to Mr. Little. He came with a great pedigree and strong marketing DNA. It took him about three months to transition from his senior executive role at a multi-national company, to our small venture of which he would become the Vice President of a department of 'one.'

With another infusion of fresh venture capital, he immediately hand-picked and recruited a direct clinical/sales organization of eight highly qualified representatives, then strategically placed each one in critical regions throughout the country. Unfortunately, after one or two false starts, the launch resulted in only modest revenues from early market adopters, and sales fell well short of the plan. (This also relates to the prior story about management 'moving the goal posts.') We tried just about everything to ignite the market, but continued to disappoint. The end-of-the-year Board Meeting approached and my Chairman indicated that they wanted to hear directly from Mr. Little as to 'why' we had stalled.

We were well-disciplined enough to always review and prep all members of the management team for their presentations to the Board of Directors, and although Mr. Little heard me tell the story multiple times, he really didn't 'listen' to the key messages. During the meeting, I set the stage as best I could and asked him to address the Board.

His story started with a pure regurgitation of my own story. No alterations, no revisions to make it his own. Glances from

the other Directors provided me with con-
firmations of my own assessment... he
was starting to sound like a hand-puppet.

Minutes into it, the Chairman raised
his hand, interrupted the flow of his story,
and asked him a series of direct questions
regarding the strategy of his decisions.
'How have you targeted and pre-qualified
customers, explain the sales cycle, and
what could be done to quickly get back on
Plan?'

Mr. Little took a deep breath, collected himself, and continued his story
from where he was interrupted. He was
attempting to stick to the fundamentals of
the story, thinking that he was 'preaching
to the choir.' Unfortunately, this audience
was no longer buying the story. He'd lost
key elements to hold them, and he wasn't
knowledgeable or quick enough on his
feet to start revising the story, to reel them
back in. Mr. Little was also extremely hon-
est to the core—a positive and negative
characteristic for a senior sales executive—
therefore he viewed 'embellishment' as on
the fringe of being deceitful.

I couldn't stand by and watch this member of my team hang himself any longer
and tried to interject... suggesting he
simply answer the key questions from

our Chairman. Rather than answer them directly, he just scrolled through the company story he'd heard dozens of times, cutting and pasting elements that he 'thought' would address the questions. It was ugly. I quickly realized he didn't have the answers. He didn't own the story. He'd lost his audience and all his credibility. The Directors' eyes were now on me, the CEO, Mr. Little's boss.

I made a feeble attempt to save him, rephrasing the questions, which included subtle elements to help direct him to a better answer... to help him construct a new creative sub-chapter in his story. He didn't get it. Frustration took over and my questions and subliminal points weren't even registering. Mr. Little's sky started to fall. Then he simply gave up.

'Listen,' he said, 'the product design isn't optimal, the use instructions need improving, and we haven't had adequate time to train our field people. If any of you have suggestions, I'm all ears and would appreciate your advice.'

My stomach did a flip. There was no saving him now. He'd not only let go of the story and lost all credibility, he'd just laid out a series of problems and questions without providing any possible solutions... a tactical error of any senior executive. He knew as well as anyone that the Board of Directors was there to help management *vet* their strategy, not *set* it. He then made the ultimate mistake of any storyteller... he asked the audience to rewrite and tell him a version of the story they would like to hear. Chicken Little's sky had truly fallen."

This is probably the best example of a storyteller who tried to stick to the fundamentals of his story, but failed at revising or embellishing certain elements when it was most important to <u>hold</u> his audience. He let it go and desperately wanted to *join* the audience and have someone else tell the story. This particular audience—the Board of Directors—had zero tolerance for an unacceptable, incomplete story and demanded that I replace this member of my team... *immediately.*

THE NUGGET:

Successful storytellers (and entrepreneurs) should realize that there will be times when they'll need to get off the path, to deviate, take a shortcut which turns out not to be necessarily shorter, but perhaps more appropriate to ensure that you'll get to your final destination. It's important to anticipate this in your journey... for many of us who tend to wander, this is inevitable. We may even get lost in the woods at times, but when it happens, just collect yourself, find a point of direction, listen for appropriate signals, and work your way back to that yellow brick road. The alternative of letting go of your story or loss of desire to get back on that road could be devastating.

CHAPTER 16

The Advanced Audience

A S OUR STORYTELLING MATURES AND ADVANCES, SO DOES our audience. Let's assume your story has attracted the necessary investors to fuel your new venture and to attract the talent that is so important to moving it forward. Regardless of your business, whether a new social media site or a state-of-art orthopedic implant, when your product eventually hits the market, new stories and strategies will be required to advance the business. You're now a seasoned storyteller and up to the task, but the audience has grown, become more complex, and many are new with very little interest or patience for the initial story.

As a founder, entrepreneur, and senior executive, you're now obligated and owe a sense of loyalty and duty to your shareholders... those who "bought" your story, believed in your value proposition, and invested in *you*. Now it's no longer about the dream, the vision or the promise... it's about optimizing a financial return on their investment. The messaging to this audience becomes even more critical, but now there's another audience that's placed in between you and your investors... the Board of Directors. This intermediary audience may be 'independent' of your shareholder audience, or a representative of certain classes. Regardless, they have been given the right to assess and even replace you! Congratulations—your storytelling abilities have just taken on an entire new meaning... personal survival.

Your intermediary audience—the Board of Directors—will be focused on both near term objectives and the longer term inflection points in your story. Structuring and communicating these components of a more sophisticated story is critical. Your continued existence as the business leader of your company depends on how well you meet these goals. Be sure they are crisp and clearly identified. This intermediary audience will have very little patience for any "fluff" or last minute excuses. Damn those goal posts!

You also need to pay attention to the larger audience *behind* those Directors—your shareholders. Fight the urge to tell them any new or revised story without first running it by your Board of Directors. I don't know of many Boards that appreciate such actions.

THE BOARD OF DIRECTORS

Nine out of ten experienced Board Members will tell you that the primary purpose of the Board is to *'hire and fire the Chief Executive Officer.'* As a founding CEO of several ventures, I've always known this to be true, but a particularly troubling concept.

Even though you created the original story... and at one point *owned* 100% of it... capital requirements brought shareholders, dilution and unfortunately the loss of majority control. Even though the story still might be yours, you now work for someone else—the Board of Directors. They now own your story, and they own *you*.

Fortunately, the Board also serves other functions than just 'hiring and firing the CEO.' Directors have a duty of care and loyalty—to be good stewards of the company. I know... at one time this was *your* company and *your* story. You're still the founder or co-founder, and that will never change, but at some point, most of us have to face the fact that it is no longer *our* company... and someone will eventually want to tell a slightly different story.

However, it's vital that you form a collaborative relationship with your Board. Not only are they your intermediary audience, but they need to properly convey your story to your most critical audience... your shareholders. Boards will spend considerable amount of time discussing how best to manage 'you,' but you must call on your best skills to properly manage *them* as well... without them realizing that you are doing so! Here are a few items you might want to tailor into your process:

- Board Members are sometimes confused over the lines of accountability.

As a business leader, you're account-able for everything. But Directors need to appreciate that you require—and deserve—a degree of autonomy... freedom to manage the day-to-day operations of your business. Keep an eye out for signs of such confu-sion and their innate desire to micro-manage certain issues. It can drive a wedge between Directors and their CEO.

- Keep your Directors informed. It's better to remind them that they've failed to open and read an emailed report from you, rather than have them criticize you for not sending one at all.

- Keeping them informed includes encouraging them to be inquisitive. An inquisitive Board is an engaged Board.

- Create a strong partnership with your Chairman—the main function of his/her role is for them to ensure there's a consensus among the Board. Without a consensus, you'll spend wasteful energy trying to pull individuals back onto your yellow brick road during the scarce and precious hours of a Board Meeting.

- Ensure your Board's actions are well-conceived and deliberate. Allowing them to make resolutions without your advanced guidance could quickly force your story off the appropriate path.

- Board agendas are extremely important and help format your story. They should be designed by mutual agreement between management and the Chairman of the Board. The agenda should be viewed as the guardrails for your meetings or calls.

- Providing Board materials prior to the meeting, should be designed to allow your Directors to analyze and critique the strategies behind your story. Again, their job does not include *setting* the strategy. If they start to set the strategy, they're taking over your story, and it probably won't be long until they start discussion a succession plan to replace you!

- This particular audience will also be responsible for understanding the assumptions behind the strategy of your story... and to assess the risks surrounding them. They will then continually monitor the quality of you and your management team's ability to execute your own strategy.

- The Board is responsible for providing performance-based compensation plans related to your strategy. This should include short-term and long-term objectives.

- Part of your strategy should include systems that oversee compliance and the appropriate metrics to help score the achievement of these objectives. This includes building a good record of your actions, results and a chronology of your communications.

THE SHAREHOLDERS

The key to telling your dynamic story to the shareholders is to now determine what they really want to know. This audience bought into your original story, but now has no interest in hearing the same old thing for the umpteenth time. They quickly evolve into the *'what have you done for me lately'* mode! It is also important for you to not simply tell them what you *think* they want to hear, but what they *need* to know to justify their original decision to support you.

In most companies, the majority of the Board—your intermediary audience—consist of representatives of these shareholders. However, once these individuals are anointed with the title, obligations and responsibility of 'Board Director,' their persona will change. They now assume they are empowered to act as mentor, advisor, judge, jury and police... but as shareholders their final objectives are all the same... to optimize company value and shareholder return on investment.

Recently there's been a shifting of regulations that is forcing the federalization of Corporate Law, moving general *Board* Governance to a *Shareholder* Governance model. In publicly-held companies, this is due to the growing presence of the 'activist shareholder.' This is a bold member of your audience who uses their equity position—regardless of the size—to put pressure on you and your story. This is the heckler in the audience.

Although they may at times make disparaging comments, and it will *feel* like a personal attack... their motives may be for various reasons. Some will be for financial reasons, seeking specific changes in your operating story—a different financing structure, cost-cutting, change in compensation plans—others may be for non-financial reasons— pushing for environmental-friendly policies or to establish a stricter cyber-security program. These activists are usually effective enough to launch a successful campaign that will push you to *at least* think about how you're going to re-tell that component of your story. They may even impact some of the core elements of your story. The sooner you get out in front of these audience members and understand their perspectives, the better prepared you'll be in addressing them.

This shareholder activism can take many forms, ranging from shareholder resolutions or proxy battles, to publicity campaigns played out in the local press. Be aware, be sensitive and figure out the best defensive measures to counteract the challenge. Deal with the issues, but try to minimize the distractions so you can stay focused on the key objectives of running the business.

THE MAD UNCLE IN THE BASEMENT

Okay, there's one other particular audience member that you need to be aware of... the one or more individuals that I've fondly come to know as 'the mad uncle in the basement.' There's usually only one, but as we all know... the one bad apple can turn others as well. This is a different type of heckler as described above.

Although this individual can be a troublesome shareholder, much different from the activist shareholder who usually becomes engaged with some form of deliberation and forethought, this individual is usually that rogue Director who acts irrationally and often times with malicious intent... for whatever reason.

With a moderate dose of paranoia, and honestly looking back at the more than a dozen Boards on which I participated, there was always 'one' guy who either fit this description or had the genetic makeup to be that mad uncle who needed to be *restrained in the basement*. He would often appear 'normal,' listening to your story with great sincerity and interest, but in his mind, it would play out differently than the others. While you had the rest of your audience focused on a certain critical element of your story, this individual would be off contemplating a twisted version of some other component. The most worrisome thing about these ordinary-appearing 'mad uncles' is that they initially seem normal but they can turn quickly, their madness surfacing at any time.

These are the audience members who would love to see you deviate from the yellow brick road... actually, some of them would enjoy seeing you flip off the road, break an axle, or even flat-out crash and burn. A dose of skepticism is healthy at times, but this is different. No one knows exactly what causes their madness; perhaps jealousy, the fear of success, or even another related compounding illness such as alcoholism. Whatever it is, if not identified and dealt with properly, they could make your life miserable by totally disrupting the flow of your story.

Like dealing with the activist shareholder above, you need to figure out a defensive mechanism to counteract their insanity as soon as it surfaces. One on one confrontations are usually not the best solution. Build a consensus with your other Directors to collectively bolt that basement door shut, or, if necessary, drag that madman from the basement and kick him to the curb!

THE NUGGET:

For advanced audiences, you'll need support and processes in place to continue telling your story, and to ensure it is told properly. Start with partnering with the Chairman of your Board. I personally think it is wise to keep the CEO and Chairman roles separated so that you broaden the team who is responsible for messaging and communication with your growing audience. Challenge your Chairman to build a consensus regarding Board-related matters. Keep your Directors engaged and make sure there's a succession plan in place to assist with replacing those who are not... and sooner if you sense any insanity.

CHAPTER 17

Selling Your Story

THERE COMES A TIME IN THE EVOLUTION OF YOUR VENTURE to SELL your story. Yes, of course, you've been *selling* that story since you first created it, but that's really "promoting"... now I mean truly selling to a new owner. For those of you who have created a lifestyle business venture for the purposes of securing a comfortable income, and perhaps turning over your company to an heir, this most likely will not apply. Feel free to advance to the next chapter. This chapter is about selling control to a buyer for the purpose of providing a return to yourself and your investors OR of liquidating assets due to insolvency.

There are a number of similar key components of the story used to raise your initial capital and the story used to harvest the value you've built in order to provide a return of capital to all involved. Obviously, the story needs to provide evidence that the venture is viable, poised for growth, and has become an established force to be reckoned with in the industry. However, you now need to include new elements of the story, most importantly... why sell now?

Selling assets due to insolvency will be dealt with later in the story, but as an example, in the event of insolvency, selling items of any value needs little explanation. When attempting to sell for any other reason, your audience is going to be suspicious about your motives. Therefore it's best to start instilling tidbits of your "exit strategy" early on, then eventually increase the emphasis as you achieve identifiable milestones that substantiate such an action.

Back in the day—that usually means when I was inexperienced and didn't know any better—it was taboo to talk about selling your company while you were just telling the story to get it off the ground. Building a company for the purpose of selling it implied you were going to take shortcuts and possibly ignore key elements that build long-term value. Today that's changed. True venture capital was designed to seed companies, partner with management, and build a solid business. This is very rare today.

Depending on your industry sector, venture capitalists will now demand to know the details of *when* and *how* you intend to provide liquidation—a return on their investment. During due diligence, I've even had a NY-based venture fund, while *considering* an investment, contact one of the market leaders in our industry to question the possibility of them acquiring my young development-stage company! Yes, times are a changing.

You should always emphasize your desire to build value for your shareholders, grow the business, take market share, and achieve specific near-term and long-term objectives. However, it also important to provide a strategy for that end-game; an initial public offering, an acquisition by one of the corporate giants, or a merger with another company that can provide the missing elements to eventually achieve one of those prior strategies.

THE SPIN

Alright, this is not bullshit, exaggeration or embellishment... although the definition could easily stimulate an argument at the local pub. Putting a different "spin" on your story is something that's now required to help you set the stage with your Board, shareholders, employees, and eventually that strategic buyer. The key to this *spin* is the timing.

At what point in your business do you believe you need to alter the story to set the stage for a sale? It's different for each company, for each founder, group of investors, and probably even for each industry. If you position this too soon, or at the wrong time, you might give the impression that you're growing weary of the challenges. Be sure to justify this new spin to your story with what might be happening in the market or within your business. Identify the issues and be sure to back them up with facts. *See... I told you it wasn't bullshit!*

"Okay, sure... I can provide several examples, but let me tell you about two very different scenarios that warranted the alteration of our story for the sole purpose of finding the right buyer.

The first involved a technology that was initially designed to accommodate the 'operating room of the future.' This was back when the first open-bore MRI—magnetic resonance imaging—systems came to the market and surgeons started contemplating doing more than just imaging for diagnostic purposes. They wanted to perform real-time surgery on patients as they were lying inside the bore of the magnet. The most interesting opportunities were associated with doing open brain surgery, the removal of brain tumors, allowing the surgeon to image and remove ALL the tiny clusters of cancerous cells which may have been left behind during conventional procedures.

The company was established to design equipment the surgeon could use inside these strong magnetic fields. Most of the normal instruments and devices were made of metals or electrical components that were not even permitted within the vicinity of an MRI scanner. It was a medical device engineer's dream come true... to convert or develop new devices that were non-ferromagnetic (i.e. plastic or ceramics) that could assist the surgeon in performing a number of different surgical procedures. Oh yeah... and since they were made of plastics, they also could be 'disposable.' The perfect business model.

Unfortunately, this new paradigm required hospitals and out-patient clinics to design new operating rooms, to physically create a surgical 'pit' at the open bore of the scanner, and to ensure that nothing in the room would be affected by the magnetic field. (A technician once accidentally wheeled in an oxygen tank that was immediately sucked into the magnetic field, causing an explosion when it slammed into the scanner, destroying the room and severely injuring everyone present. We also witnessed the destruction of many cameras and cell phones during those early years.)

Obviously, this market was slow to evolve, so this little company had to figure out how to adapt its novel technology to another application to survive. With a few quick design modifications and the engagement of a few new product champions, devices were built to optimize the placement of electrodes deep into the brain to treat Parkinson's disease. This newly FDA-approved procedure was slowly emerging, but still done in the conventional operating room. The story was altered, team re-focused, and all worked hard at staying on that bumpy, twisty and slippery yellow brick road.

Unfortunately, at the time, there was only ONE company marketing an FDA cleared product for Deep Brain Neurostimulation. It became obvious that we needed to partner with this company if we wanted to survive. Reality followed closely behind... they were also the one and only buyer of the company. The only viable way to get our shareholders a return on their investment.

The challenge of 'spinning' our story was to convince this large corporation that they needed us more than we needed them! This also required us to spin our tale differently to our shareholders to get their support of what later became a staged acquisition. Unfortunately, this forced us to pursue the scariest of all directives... to put all of our eggs in one basket. To make matters worse, we were running out of capital and our venture capital inves-tors were either tapped out or getting *deal fatigue*—the point where it was becoming a real effort for them to continue with us on our journey. The well had dried up.

Our team became experts in this particular procedure, knowing it as well, if not better, than many of the surgeons or the supplier of the pulse generator and electrodes used to treat the patient. We found the Achilles heel of the procedure and focused on enhancing our solution. Months later we had the opportunity to tell our tale to this corporate giant—not only enlightening them of a problem, the size and scope of which they were not really aware of, but providing them with the solution as well. We appeared as their knights in shining white armor and they'd eventually agree to accommodate our financing needs IF and only IF they could own the company at a certain period of time in the defined future... conditional upon achieving certain success.

The next step was to now convince the Board and our shareholders that it was the appropriate time to consider such an acquisition offer. We were stepping way off of the intended path, the goal posts were moved, but we spun a tale that provided no other tangible alternative. It was time to *sell the bitch* ("STB").

Yes, that one ended pretty well. Investors received somewhere between two to three times their investment in a reasonably short period of time. It wasn't a home-run, but a good solid double. Timing was everything.

As an alternative to that story, I've been involved in another venture in which the decision to identify an exit was driven by a completely different set of circumstances. The spin was a bit more elaborate and as of the writing of these words, the outcome still unsure.

Remember the story told back in Chapter 3 about the development of that 'autofocusing' implantable lens? Well, after years of development with the best engineers scattered throughout the U.S. and Europe, the initial device was now ready for manufacturing. The stage was set for a clinical study to support the commercial approval in Europe—the first critical milestones for any implantable medical device—clinical validation followed by proof of market acceptance.

The company had managed to pull together the millions of dollars needed for the design and development of its first product. Perhaps another million or more was spent on securing all the patents necessary to protect such a complex device. Additional venture capital was extremely rare and very expensive. Private equity and angel investors were becoming 'tapped out.' All at the worst possible time... we needed double what we'd raised to date in order to kick off a very complex fabrication process including vendors and assemblers from Holland to India. It was time to spin a new tale.

Fortunately, the technology had a built in story component that provided some relief—from a storyteller's point of view. All the proprietary components, i.e. the secret sauce, were sealed in a thin wafer that was then encapsulated into a normal, conventional lens that is commonly implanted in the eyes of all cataract patients. The company had developed its own high quality conventional lens in which these electronics would be inserted; similar to INTEL Inside. If we partnered with one of the market leaders in the U.S., Europe or Japan, we could eliminate many of the redundancies in our manufacturing process and reduce the overall capital required to move this forward... capital which would be dilutive to all the shareholders. All true, but there was the spin.

We'd put everything on hold—not necessarily telling everyone that we HAD to put things on hold due to the absence of any additional funding sources—but because we deliberately and systematically wanted to assess the opportunities of partnering in order to optimize the costs and time to market. We positioned ourselves as searching for a "partner" which in realty meant we needed to sell the company sooner than later. It wasn't an exaggeration (or bullshit), all was true, not even an embellishment... the story was simply spun in such a way that met the needs of all interested parties. The end... and I'm sticking to that story."

THE NUGGET:

In today's economic environment and new slog of investors, focused on getting in on the next social media fad or mobile app for a quick return on their investment, its critical to map out your exit strategy sooner than later. However, be cautious and deliberate when constructing an alternative ending to your story... you may only have one or two chances to do so. In doing so too often, you'll appear careless, even reckless... stepping off the yellow brick road looking for cover... and dodging flying monkeys!

CHAPTER 18

Holding on to a Lost Art

STORYTELLING IS BECOMING A LOST ART THAT WE NEED TO revive and emphasize to expand entrepreneurism throughout the world. From the perspective of an old-school, med-tech entrepreneur—that's me—there seems to be a segregation of technologies requiring different storytelling skills. The industries that I've grown up with require a level of business discipline that doesn't seem to be that critical for the virtual world of internet technologies. Don't get me wrong, those youngsters who develop social media sites and cyber gaming are extremely bright... and we can't deny the existence of new multi-billion dollar industries since Mr. Gates and Mr. Jobs opened up a whole new universe. It's just that an idea to create a website where people can exchange pictures and chat about their day requires a different type of storytelling to get it funded than, say, a description of a targeted nano-therapy to treat a malignant brain tumor.

Our *investor* audiences tend to be attracted to certain business opportunities because of their backgrounds, education, professions, and/or personal experiences. A commercial pilot, for example, will be most interested in considering a private investment in a new aviation business but he'd probably scratch his head over the revenue model proposed by the next Facebook venture. Therefore it is essential to not only seek out the most appropriate audience for your story, but to make sure you tell the story well. There's a difference in being a *strong* storyteller and a *powerful* one. Being powerful implies you're delivering the message with a sense of conviction and drive. Be powerful!

Regardless of what business you wish to create, there are essential elements that every audience needs to hear in your story. Don't just lay these items out there as if you're providing them with a checklist. Show your conviction and sincerity when describing each one.

- **Investors need to see evidence of a business leader with a proven track record.** This isn't the time to be humble or bashful. Tell them how great you are, even if you haven't had the ability to show such greatness in businesses that relate to your new venture. Draw correlations from other experiences. Convince them you have the ability, drive and conviction to see it through. Be powerful.

- **They need to know that you can build an experienced management team.** Do your homework here. Identify the key team members you'll need to move the technology forward. Perhaps even go as far as mention specific people with whom you've meet, plan to recruit, and even steal away from other organizations. Show that you know what it takes to incentivize and retain these supporting characters.

- **Your audience needs to understand your plan of operations and how much and how long it will take to complete.** That's right. Not only do you have to explain why you believe your new great idea is necessary and how you can impact the current market, but you need to justify how you'll use their investment dollars to build the enterprise. Show them specific "inflection points" (milestones) that will drive value in the business— when they will occur and what it's going to take to achieve them. Just be careful… you'll eventually be measured against these milestones to assess your performance. Be powerful… but be careful.

- **They'll expect you to know the intricate details of the market.** Again... do your homework. Don't just stop at reading market reports. Get out there and talk with customers, get to know the competition, and provide a comparison of the pros and cons of each. Show no mercy in explaining why your idea is optimal over the competition.

- **Is it a game-changer or just a better mousetrap?** The term 'go big or go home' might be overused, but may be appropriate here. Your audience is looking for something big, a homerun. Even if your concept is just a novel improvement over what's currently available, you'll need to find something that differentiates your product from the conventional norm. Make it stand out, even if it only involves a creative marketing scheme that hasn't been used. Go big... stand out!

Today's brave new world includes virtual companies in dynamic markets that are evolving every six months, not six years. Founders are often young, inexperienced—yet usually highly intelligent—individuals who pitch from iPads and provide three page executive summaries. Regardless of the business, the genius behind it, the paradigm-shift in technology... they all, without exception, require the necessary components of powerful storytelling to push them over the top.

If you feel unsure of yourself or your ability to tell the story, go sit in the audience every chance you get. Hone your skills as a listener, track the success of those telling the story and correlate the components of their story with the evolution of their business. Study the Art. It has a history, and a future that will never end.

THE NUGGET:

Strive to perfect the Art of Storytelling. Once you do, be sure to mentor and help others to continue the art. Start with your key employees. Join the Boards of other companies and become engaged with their messaging and communication of their vision and corporate mission. Hold on to the Art.

CHAPTER 19

Once Upon a Time

YOU'RE NOW ENTERING THE LARGEST CHAPTER OF THIS adventure, which I've broken down into sub-chapters, each providing a glimpse into the stimulus that drove my desire to establish a new company and tell my story. You'll recognize links to certain tidbits I've used in prior chapters. As I just previously stated, try to build on your experiences, intertwine your stories when possible, and learn from the 'good, bad and ugly.'

Collectively, I've raised over $260 million to start and grow these businesses from family, friends, private investors and venture funds. Looking back on this collection of ten (10) selected stories, it really warrants starting with, "Once upon a time..."

Story #1 – Breaking into the Business

I was a young man, freshly plucked out of graduate school before I would even finish my studies in an advanced scientific field. What I'd learned and practiced became sufficient to provide at least some initial degree of credibility in the medical device industry. My first publication and patent application had caught the eye of a large private device manufacturer in the Midwest and I was thrown into a business environment that I never knew existed. I either independently picked up the knowledge or was trained by more seasoned executives on the foundations of business and how to design, develop, manufacture and market medical devices. After nearly six years of *workin' for the man*, I became armed and dangerous; armed with a depth of knowledge in every aspect of the business, and dangerous with the drive to do it on my own... to be an entrepreneur and leader of my own company. I was then twenty-eight years old.

The Midwest company was a world-class interventional device company that developed, manufacturing, and marketed catheter systems to both the radiologist and cardiologist. My primary task was to educate other physicians as to the benefits of these procedures, and to determine how they could be adapted to their clinical applications... to tell the story. Along the way, we established a new division in the Critical Care markets and developed over forty new devices and related procedures.

About the same time, a new material was introduced by a Japanese competitor that had an enormous impact in the market. I then did another dangerous thing... I fell in love with the technology. It was a new shape-memory, super-elastic alloy that could be formed and shaped into various devices. NITINOL ("ni-tin-ol") was a unique blend of nickel and titanium which provided dozens of benefits over the conventional stainless-steel used in medical devices. As expected, this privately-owned innovative company jumped right in with both feet and started to explore various short-term and long-term projects that incorporated the use of these new sexy materials.

My personal thoughts and ideas on where it might be used became just an irritating *noise* within this organization. They weren't totally ignored, but they were viewed as either over-challenging, or too innovative and risky—requiring a new regulatory approval and marketing strategy. They were simply looking at converting existing stainless-steel devices over to this new material; devices that were core to their existing business.

I then read about a small company in Minneapolis that was using this new material in the orthodontics market, developing an 'arch wire'—dental braces— that would move the patient's teeth at a greater, more predictable rate than using titanium or stainless wires. A field-trip was all it took to further convince me that I had to be involved in the exploitation of this new material.

This Minneapolis-based company then introduced me to their largest investor, another privately-held company in Wisconsin focused on custom plastic injection molding. This company had built a reputation for high quality and state-of-the-art molding capabilities and was producing everything ranging from sleek Saab dashboards and nifty Polaroid cameras—remember, this was *back in the day*—to novel disposable medical instruments. They were deep-pocketed and had a burning desire to diversify into the medical industry. The first phase of their strategy was to make equity investments into new companies that would benefit from their design and manufacturing expertise.

The President of the orthodontics business made the introduction. During my first visit to their Technology Center, their fatherly-like CEO who seemed to ignore my youth and limited experience, asked me if I had a business plan that I would like to submit. I didn't, but promised one anyway. During the short flight back home that afternoon, I crafted an outline of my first story... one using this new precious alloy in various non-existing devices for small tortuous vessels where no other systems seemed to work due to limitations in existing materials. My first company was born three months later; **MICROVENA**—indicating "small vessel applications." Our focus would be in pediatrics, cardiology and neurology. I learned quickly how to tell the story.

MICROVENA was an enlightening and painful experience. We went on to raise very little equity and somehow managed to advance the company using debt financing from this 'parent' company in Wisconsin. I was rather inexperienced at the time and given the opportunity, I would have done it differently... but that's another story, another book.

As the company became more successful, and more valuable, our equity and debt financing partners become more interested—AND greedier. Nearly ten years after its birth, this Wisconsin-based company, for a variety of personal and unprofessional reasons still unknown today, exercised its option to convert the debt to equity, took majority control, changed the Board and sold the company to a large private equity firm; which later took the company public. Yes, that fatherly-like CEO eventually turned into the mad uncle in the basement! Fortunately, most of the technology and products are still used in treating patients today all over the world.

Story #2 – A Novel Coronary By-Pass Procedure

Nearly four years into the creation of MICROVENA, the company was successfully commercializing several unique Nitinol-based devices both in the fields of Interventional Radiology and Cardiology. It was a rare, warm spring morning when I met with a cardiologist-turned-businessman in my Minnesota office—requesting my time to hear his own story.

He'd seen and read about our novel technologies and had an idea for a completely new set of devices for a specific procedure. He asked me if we'd consider licensing his NEWCO some of our intellectual property and know-how in exchange for a significant equity position in the new venture. This was way off our radar and our little company, with my younger self at the helm, needed to stay focused. However, the technology whore inside me was interested and needed to learn more. We signed a Non-disclosure Agreement and agreed to have a working session in my office later that week.

The idea was off the charts! We'd be absolutely crazy to consider it, which further drove my desire to be a part of it. I helped him create the proper story that we needed to pitch to the big money guys in Wisconsin, as well as the rest of my Board in order to seek approval in "licensing" our technology to another newly formed entity. We finally agreed to license specific patents for a specific field of use to this NEWCO in exchange for a 30% ownership position. I'd also disclosed that I would be receiving additional founding shares, planned to make a small investment, and would sit on their Board of Directors.

The idea was to use the super-elastic and thermal/shape-memory features of Nitinol to develop a catheter-based system to perform a cardiac bypass procedure on a beating heart. At the time, nearly every bypass procedure was being done surgically, while the patient was put on a heart-lung bypass machine, with the heart temporarily in a suspended state. Several companies were attempting to perform a 'minimally-invasive' procedure through ports and small incisions in the chest, but this would be the first attempt at doing a blind (closed-chest) procedure in the Cardiac Cath Lab through various catheters—on a beating heart, while the patient was awake and conversing with the clinician.

We identified eight technology challenges and started to file additional independent patents to protect specific key elements of both the methods and devices that would be required. The goal: to pull together an experienced engineering/development team to build the devices and obtain 'clinical validation' of the system in a human study, most likely somewhere outside of the United States.

This Cardiologist and I both had full-time "day jobs," therefore it was important for us to identify and recruit a business leader... a solid *professional manager* with experience and a track-record in the industry... and most importantly, an entrepreneurial spirit, willing to take the leap of faith to help us raise the necessary capital. We put together the essence of our story and went hunting for our next audience member. We found him, semi-retired, on a golf-course in Arizona. We set the hook and reeled him in.

While the lawyers filed the corporate foundation documents, we drafted the technology development plan and supplemented it with the most current market data we could find. The plan identified the staging of the eight critical components, materials and fixtures needed to build prototypes, and the engineering talent required to expedite the plan. We had a budget.

It dictated that we'd need approximately seven million dollars to reach our primary objective: proof of concept in a human subject. We were too early, too risky for venture capital. We needed to mitigate the technology and clinical risks before they'd be interested. Understood and appreciated. Therefore, we tightened up our story and prepared a series of flipcharts that included a list of key bullet points, engineering drawings and graphs. *Microsoft PowerPoint was just recently launched and we hadn't figure out how to optimize its value yet.* We then went out on the road to raise the money... one investor at a time.

We approached the obvious audience members who we thought would have an appreciation for our story—the interventional cardiologist. It was during a time when the market was exploding with new technology surrounding balloon angioplasty and vascular stents... these guys were printing money and had an appetite for more innovation!

These docs also weren't shy about their views on our story. They either loved it or hated it, not much in between. Regardless of their opinion, we incorporated their comments and views into enhancing our story. It became more powerful with each meeting. We eventually raised the required capital in two phases, and decided to start testing 'components' of our complicated procedural devices in different surgical procedures. Seeking validation of our components was meant to provide confidence in the big-picture story... but we never got there. One of the key implantable devices was designed to lock in a temporary vascular conduit, to support a vein graft for the by-pass procedure. It worked well... extremely well.

Word got out to a major company in Minnesota about the effectiveness of this implantable 'anastomotic device' that would benefit one of their existing surgical procedures. A handsome offer was made, and the company, **Vascular Science**, was acquired within three years of its creation. Those participating audience members received approximately fourteen times their investment.

Story #3 – Developing Embryonic Stem Cells

As it often happens, a friend-of-a-friend... in this case a *brother-of-a-friend*, approached me with another opportunity. Given my undergraduate studies in biochemistry and cytology, this new bio-technology opportunity piqued my interest. The friend's brother was a well-known, award-winning scientist who had actually been involved with the cloning of Dolly, the sheep in Scotland. Now managing a human genetic engineering laboratory at a prestigious university in the Southeast, this entrepreneurial scientist told me a compelling story of his next adventure. What they needed was help in structuring a company around their technology... someone who would help construct the story and raise capital beyond the grant money they'd already secured.

I'm terrible at saying "no," so off we went, arm-in-arm, skipping off onto that yellow brick road. This journey, however, once again started with my own need to be educated. Several visits to their laboratory finally provided me with the pieces needed to construct the appropriate story, along with that ever-pressing Executive Summary.

In 1999, it was at the precipice of a new technology known as Stem Cell Therapy. The main story was about using healthy, vibrant clusters of embryonic cells that can be transplanted in specific areas of the body to stimulate the production of a missing chemical, enzyme, protein, hormone, or biochemical process to repair a physiological function that had been damaged or depleted. This was viewed as a potential 'cure' for diseases ranging from Diabetes to Parkinson's.

The special sauce of this new venture would be the process of cloning and growing these precious cells. They needed an optimal environment to cultivate a viable quantity that could then be inserted into the core of specific organs, where this cluster of new cells could thrive, survive and do their job. Patents were filed on the use of human epithelial cells—skin cells—that would serve as the fertile ground on which these delicate cells would be planted and grown. Competitors were using various animal cell layers for this purpose, causing concerns over cross-contamination of human and animal cellular components. The bed of human skin cells would ensure these 'human stem cells' would flourish without fear of any infection from impurities.

In order to properly tell the story, we had to address a critical controversial component—right up front. There was no sugar coating it. The source of the human stem cells during this time period (1999-2003) came from discarded human embryos that were created in the wombs of women seeking impregnation from in vitro fertilization. Clinicians would stimulate their bodies with hormones to create numerous eggs which would be extracted, fertilized in a petri dish, and reinserted in hopes that the embryos would be accepted by her body and sustained as a healthy pregnancy. The other half dozen fertilized embryos would be frozen and stored in liquid nitrogen in the event the initial implants wouldn't take. If successful, the remaining embryos would be discarded—or in this case, used for research purposes. During this time, federal and state regulators were just trying to understand the science behind embryonic stem cells and the public wasn't far behind them. Activists soon surfaced and the story's complexity grew due to sensitivity with potential investors. Our audience started to shrink.

As Chairman of this young company, my exposure was high, and therefore I had become very engaged in working with management to ensure the messaging was 'right and tight.' However, there was no way in getting around what we were actually doing... using in vitro fertilized embryos to harvest human stem cells.

In August 2001, then President George W. Bush imposed a moratorium on federal funding of embryonic stem cell research. Fortunately, Bush's policy allowed research using human embryonic stem cells if certain criteria was met. Our laboratory was one of fourteen research groups that were recognized to have met this criteria and we seemed to have successfully navigated through the woods and found ourselves back on the yellow brick road.

However, regardless of how we perfected our story, we still had lost the majority of our audience... regardless of 'blessings' from federal regulators. The goal of the company to 'cure' certain diseases was commendable, but the story was too controversial. We couldn't raise a nickel from institutional investors.

Other laboratories outside the U.S., in India, Israel, Singapore, Sweden and South Korea accelerated the race to develop these valuable embryonic stem cells, but we still had a proprietary piece of the puzzle. We solicited funds from insiders, family and friends while seeking a corporate partnership with a non-U.S. company who might appreciate the value of our special sauce. Eventually our story resonated with a publicly-traded company in Australia. They'd been working on similar processes for different applications and the combination of the two companies was viewed as a match made in heaven. The next challenge was to properly blend the stories given the added complexity of two companies at opposite ends of the globe, the cultural differences, and certain redundancies in management.

Given the list of assets and perceived value of both companies, it was agreed that our little private venture would need to bring additional working capital to a proposed 50:50 merger. Cash was already scarce, but the opportunity to 'merge' with a publicly-traded biotechnology company—even though it was on the Australian exchange—provided us with a new element of our story that potential investors might warm up to. Unfortunately, this wasn't the case.

We struggled with what now became a very complicated story, a technology shrouded with controversy, a U.S. management team that would most likely be replaced by the Australian team, and lack of clarity on how investors might be able to successfully liquidate their shares on the Australian exchange. We didn't have much of a choice... either die a slow death over the next ten years chasing research grants, or take a chance on getting to a closing with our new Australian colleagues.

We somehow pulled together the mandated two million dollars in additional capital—yes, thanks to all those family, friends and home equity loans—and closed the merger about nine months later. Two of the Co-founders/Directors of our small Board were required to serve as Directors on the merged company's Board of Directors down under. During my first long flight to Adelaide, Australia, I started to craft my notes in preparation for the new story that would be told to the local Press upon my arrival. Little did I know that it was only the beginning of another long journey replete with flying monkeys and several mad uncles in the basement... but that's a whole new story! We eventually arrived at Emerald City and **Cytogenesis**—our little biotech venture—was successfully merged with BresaGen

Ltd. Less than two years later, the newly merged entity was acquired by another large Australian biotechnology company. Developments for a 'cure' are still underway to this day.

Story #4 – Treating Restenosis of Coronary Stents

Why can't I say 'no'? It must be an illness or an addiction. Does anyone know of a rehab center for entrepreneurs? Please email me! Here's one of those stories you won't find detailed on my resume. There's no happy ending here (yet) and it's still wandering down a long yellow brick road filled with detours and littered with casualties along its path.

The call came from a long-time business partner, fellow entrepreneur and friend in Germany. He'd identified a technology that could be a game-changer in the newly emerging arena taking the cardiology market by storm. Several companies had developed and successfully commercialized a device that could be placed in the diseased, narrowed vessels of the heart to keep them open... a coronary stent. These small coils were permanently expanded and embedded in the walls of these delicate heart vessels. Unfortunately, often months later, the device would stimulate the natural cascade of clots that would form around this foreign body sitting up against the vessel wall. The occlusive blood clots—thrombus—would eventually expand to the point of causing a similar narrowing; a phenomenon known as *restenosis*.

My German friend became aware of a new technology that could treat these metallic stents from *outside* the body without the need of another intervening procedure. As more stents were placed in hearts all over the world, the prevalence of this problem grew exponentially. A solution was needed and the answer was sitting in a laboratory in a German university hospital, waiting to be unleashed.

We put together a plan to license the technology from the university and engaged another experienced German engineer/businessman who would push the development of the technology forward as a critical member of the team. We pulled in another finance guy—whom we knew and trusted—and with management and technology secured, I set off to incorporate the company and draft yet another exciting story. One more U.S. start-up company was born.

This story would be easy to tell. It included an elegant solution to a rapidly growing problem. Inexpensive and non-invasive, it only required a bit of development work, a quick clinical study to prove safety and efficacy, and then a sale to highest bidding company in the Cardiology market.

For all you techie readers, this solution used an old, well-understood principle of magnetic fields. The implanted stent sitting inside of the vessel was made of a specific alloy that would serve as an internal receiving coil for a pulsed magnetic wave. The company developed a hand-held magnet using a specifically tuned, pulsed frequency that would cause heating of the stent from a physical process known as magnetic hysteresis. Controls were built into the system, based on the type, size and location of the stent, that would heat the stent to a very specific temperature—sufficient to destroy the newly formed clots *and* to gently scar the lining of the vessel so no new occlusions would return. All of this could be theoretically accomplished by a hand-held device outside of the body on a patient sitting in the doctor's office. The competition was attempting to develop a variety of therapeutic treatments that required an intervention with new catheters, balloons and wires being inserted into the patient's heart. We convinced ourselves that we had another tiger by the tail!

We relocated our German engineer to the States, pulled together the presentation materials and hit the road to tell our compelling story. We wouldn't need much capital or a large team to pull this off, but little did we know how many of those flying monkeys were hiding up in the trees.

One of the market leaders in the stent business announced they were developing their own solution... a coating on the stent that would *inhibit* this restenosis. It was bound to the surface using a special polymer that would slowly release an inhibitory drug over time. Our sphincters tightened as our initial audiences told us they were going to 'wait and see' if such a coating would actually work—data was promised to be released within the next several months.

At the time, the drugs being used to coat these stents were not proven for such applications, so we altered our story and went on the attack, trying to convince our audience that systemic effects would be unknown and hard to assess, and that the FDA would take years to approve such a coating. Regardless of whether our story was right or wrong, we couldn't compete with the marketing machines of the larger companies who were working hard to protect their stent franchise. Our novel solution no longer sounded interesting... or necessary. We no longer could find an audience who even wanted to hear our story.

Story #5 – A Nanotechnology for Targeted Cancer Therapy

As many entrepreneurs will tell you, it's hard... if not impossible... to roll over and play dead. Our small team described in the previous story, regrouped and set off to identify another application for our technology. It was really the first time we found ourselves with a *technology that needed a home*. Fortunately, members of our small management team had developed an expanded business network throughout both Europe and the U.S. and we were soon in front of executives who were leading other larger companies—explaining the value of our protected, platform technology.

One particular private company, based in the Boston area, had successfully developed and commercialized a number of novel nanotechnologies for the industrial and military/defense markets. They now wanted to diversify in the healthcare, medical device industry by merging their nano-biotechnology with our pulsed magnetic heating company which we've since renamed **Thermonix**. Their story included a big hook that grabbed and held our attention, and we spent the next couple of months finalizing a merger agreement that pushed us off onto another yellow brick road.

The combined technologies would chase the holy grail of medical device applications—a treatment for cancer that would obsolete the need for chemo or radiation therapy. Okay, we may have embellished the story a bit there... it would at least *minimize* the need for these other therapies. Time, money and clinical trials would help us prove whether or not we could eliminate these other harsh treatments.

Preliminary meetings with the FDA indicated that they would regulate this new therapy as a medical device, not a biological agent or drug, therefore the merged NEWCO would require our management and financing expertise in the medical device industry. I was asked to be Chairman and since I had not yet checked into that rehab center, I hadn't yet mastered the ability to say, "No, thank you."

Armed with combined biotech and medical device experiences, this was an easy and exciting story to tell. The new company would use the concept of heating a microscopic internal alloy (metal) inside the body using the external hand-held magnet of Thermonix. The pulsed magnetic waves would cause sufficient heating to destroy the cancer cells. The complicated part of the story was explaining the new receiving element... it was no longer just a coil of metal sitting inside the vessel wall. It would be something the world hadn't seen before.

The Boston-based company developed a method to produce nano-particles of iron oxide—rust particles. However these microscopic particles were of uniform size and density and had a special magnetic quality that allowed for the controlled heating by the magnetic field. These particles became our 'payload'... the killer-probe that would be heated to over four hundred degrees to ablate the cancer cells. We then needed to use a biological component that would specifically target the cancer... to carry our little secret weapon and attach it to the surface of the malignant cells.

There was a growing source of antibodies being developed by other large biotech/pharma companies throughout the world, but it was a numbers game. Companies developed scores of antibodies to test which one would have any 'therapeutic effect.' It was a small percentage. The rest of the antibodies, like those unused fertilized embryos at Cytogenesis, were placed on the shelf, each having a mountain of clinical data regarding their specificity and targeting capabilities... they simply had no therapeutic power.

We crafted a story to tell these big pharma companies, one showing how we could blow the dust off of their 'non-therapeutic antibodies' and offer some value to what they've already spent millions of dollars to develop. Our little company produced a technique to 'conjugate' (attach) their antibodies to our small particles of iron. These antibodies were specific to certain cancers; breast, lung or prostate cancer cells. The technology represented aggressive elements of *seek and destroy* and therefore was referred to as "targeted nano-therapy" —the TNT Project.

We licensed an antibody that was specific to breast cancer, conjugated it with our nano-particles of iron and showed how the antibodies would carry the particles and bind to the surface of the cancer cells. We would then activate the pulsed magnetic field which caused extreme heating of these tiny particles, punching holes in the cancer cells, killing them without effecting an adjacent healthy cell. We pushed aside thoughts of the Holy Grail as visions of the Nobel Prize danced in our heads. But as my wife would often say, "Whoa... not so fast, Sparky!"

Taking the story on the road, we were stunned—no, actually shocked—by the response. Of those investors who might consider investing in a combined biotech/medical device play, only a handful had experience in the treatment of cancer. We quickly discovered that such therapies were not supported by many venture investors. This was an industry that was funded by research grants, philanthropists, and internal funds within large pharma/biotech companies.

There were too many casualties alongside the road, too much capital wasted on therapies that failed late in clinical trials when pivotal data was uncovered. We were way too early to show any proof of concept in man, and therefore not financeable. Another dead end. More hard lessons learned.

We disbanded the team, paid off our expenses, and locked up the intellectual property in a cabinet; some of which I'd attempt to pursue later for

a unique orthopedic application to treat osteoar-
thritic pain—another story told here, but not in this
chapter. Fortunately, less than a year later, several
key shareholders identified a California-based biotech company that found value in several of our
remaining assets. Another merger was formed and
our NEWCO—**Triton BioSystems**—was merged
with Oncologics to form another viable ongoing
venture called Aduro Biotech. Our equity participation was converted and we're now skipping down
yet another yellow brick road. Although this group
struggles with *going along for the ride*, we're now following others who are leading the way to develop a
targeted immunotherapy for pancreatic cancer.

Story #6 – Parkinson's Disease – A Procedural Solution

One of the problems with starting an early career as an entrepreneur is that, whether you're successful or not, at some point you'll depart that exciting venture that got you out of bed at 5:00 A.M. every morning and find yourself wondering 'what's next.'

I'd just exited two ventures within twenty-four months and was looking to relocate to Florida for personal/family reasons when I received a call from a local, well-respected Venture Capital fund. They asked if I'd be interested in joining the Board of Directors on a new company they were forming with licensed patents from the University of Minnesota. Within a month of accepting the directorship, they then asked... or rather insisted... that I become the company's CEO. *Go ahead, say 'no'... I dare ya!*

After informing the investors and small Board of Directors that I had plans for moving to Florida, they responded by telling me to take the company with me. I had already explored the market opportunity, learned the fundamentals of the technology and visited with the founders at the University on multiple occasions. With initial capital already sitting in the bank, it was an easy decision. While other family members looked for a rental home in Florida, I stayed back to craft yet another Executive Summary and slide deck... the main purpose, to recruit key employees in a new region of the country where I knew absolutely no one. The first call was to that friend and former Chief Operating Officer that I mention in the previous Chapter 4. He not only helped me craft the final pieces of my story, but by the end of the conversation, he'd become my first employee.

My next audience would be other potential employees. I had stepped into a new environment with no existing network and just engaged a regional recruiting firm to line up dozens of interviews with prospective engineers, quality inspectors, bookkeepers, and administrative personnel. They'd made arrangements for a large conference room at the beachside Radisson Hotel in Melbourne, Florida—the middle of the Spacecoast, just south of Cape Canaveral. The room was filled with eager, highly qualified individuals who were either unemployed or already given notices that their jobs at the space center was being eliminated.

We decided to provide the group with an introduction and overview of the Company and what we intended to achieve. My story was simplified and also focused on how the medical device industry designed, developed, tested and commercialized a product. Without exception, none of the audience members had ever heard such a story. The fact that their potential work could be inserted or attached to the human body for the sake of improving someone's quality of life was all the hook that I needed.

We then simply had to select the cream of the crop and to properly train them.

The selection process was more difficult than the training. I had under-estimated the sophistication of this audience. The majority had worked for NASA or one of the many local aviation or telecommunications companies that had sprouted throughout the region. The product we intended to initially design was described to them as a "skull-mounted GPS device for the neurosurgeon." I didn't need to teach any of these folks about navigation or telemetry. What they were hungry for was information about how stock options worked, and what kind of documentation control was necessary. I adjusted my story and reeled them in.

As previously described, this operating room of the future that included an open-field magnet—an MRI system—was slow to develop. The capital equipment, new MRI machine, and renovation costs for building these rooms escalated to millions of dollars. Our little company was proficiently designing and building a family of new commercially available devices... FDA approvals were easily achieved... and we were sitting at the edge of a new paradigm-shift for surgical procedures requiring our technology. What we did *not* plan on was a downturn in the economy, reduced reimbursement for procedures and equipment, and a tightening of hospital budgets. We needed to redefine ourselves and come up with yet another new story.

We had too much capital invested in product development and regulatory approvals, it therefore would have been too tough to tell a story that not only included moving the goal posts, but stopping the game at half-time to play rugby rather than football. We quickly hit the road to see if there was another clinical application for our products. Three weeks later, we were crafting a different story that included an image-guided surgical procedure that could be performed in existing operating rooms. A major pacemaker company had just received FDA clearance to market a brain pacemaker to treat Parkinson's disease. The initial procedure was barbaric and screaming for a solution... a solution that required a slight tweak in our current products. We had ourselves a new story to tell.

These poor patients had to have a small section of their skull removed and required a stainless steel frame to be literally bolted to their head, which in turn was attached to the surgical table. The frame was used to immobilize their heads and to provide a protractor-like means to determine the geographical location of a specific target deep in their brain.

To assess the effectiveness of the electrodes that would be used to "regulate" the misfiring of their brainwaves causing the symptoms of their disease, these patients had to be temporarily taken off their medications. They were awake during the entire procedure which would often take eight to ten hours to complete.

We told the tale of a new *procedural solution*, one that would eliminate the need to bolt their heads to a frame, minimize the opening in their skull, provide equal or greater accuracy, reduce risks associated with the procedure, and most-importantly, reduce the procedure time down to less than ninety minutes.

This story resonated well with everyone, including the large manufacturer of the brain pacemaker (neurostimulator). This company provided the last round of financing needed to commercialize this *procedural solution*, and we negotiated a specific set of milestones that would allow them to acquire our company, **Image-guide NEUROLOGICS**, at a pre-agreed upon acquisition price. We achieved the milestones and closed the transaction less than a year later.

Story #7 – Early Diagnosis of Skin Cancer

An element of this story was discussed in Chapter 13, but more details might be warranted to provide proper exposure to what I've come to know as the *good, bad* and *ugly* in my career. Unfortunately, this pushed the terminal end of that scale.

Networking. This is critical to any entrepreneur regardless of industry sector. I had been diligently working as the CEO of another company in Florida, keeping my head down, staying focused. To minimize travel, I started to reject offers to speak at venture conferences beyond the Southeast region. I'd agreed to present at the Florida Venture Forum where it was also known that I was being considered as a nominee for the Ernst & Young Entrepreneur of the Year Award. Most of the audience had heard my story before, but I had now become a target of interest by law firms, executive recruiters and regional investment bankers.

Following my presentation, I walked towards one of the multiple exits from the large ballroom that opened into the foyer filled with exhibitors. Coffee stations were strategically positioned to pull attendees through a gauntlet of company representatives, each eager to pitch their own stories. Reaching for a clean mug, I was intercepted by a familiar face who was just recently sitting in the front row. He was a well-established corporate attorney with a prestigious firm in W. Palm Beach. Again, I was asked if I had a minute to learn more about a local healthcare company he was recently retained to assist. They had just incorporated and were looking to add a seasoned med-tech Director to their Board. *Come on... you can do it... just say 'no!'*

Obviously, this attorney—now friend of mine—was a proficient storyteller of his own. By the end of the following week, I was pouring through materials only to realize that I was indeed *hooked* once again. The technology story needed a great deal of improvement and I immediately saw where and how I could possibly add value. A call to another Minnesota-based friend to discuss how the technology might apply to his own diagnosis of melanoma—skin cancer—just set the hook even deeper. It could have changed his life and how he manages this disease.

The technology was being spun-out of another industrial/agricultural business, with the original founder expanding an existing application used for military surveillance. During the Vietnam War, they suspended cameras underneath the belly of helicopters that could visualize biological materials using a patented hyper-spectral imaging system. We've all seen those infra-red images of glowing bodies running for cover from airplanes over terrorist camps, but this system was sensitive enough to ascertain whether or not they were American or

Vietnamese soldiers based on the biological signatures of their skin.

A new company was being formed around the ability to scan a patient's entire body to determine whether or not skin cancer cells were developing beneath the surface BEFORE they became visible by the naked eye. Just months prior, the National Cancer Institute made a statement that if skin cancer could be diagnosed early enough, people would no longer die from skin cancer. Living in Florida, with multiple new spots emerging everywhere on my body, I was sold—sign me up!

We tightened up the story with images of cancerous cells found underneath the skin, with no visible signs of discoloration on the surface. A prototype scanner that would slide inches over the patient on a standard chair or examination table would add to the credibility of the tale. We now just needed some additional human data points to show it was efficacious.

We pitched our story to a local dermatologist who had a three to four month wait list of patients wanting to have their sun spots and/or moles examined. Visions of patients walking through a future scanner to triple his thru-put danced in his head. We lined up a quick study in which the patient would be scanned, early un-detectable clusters of cells would be biopsied and proven to be cancerous before they even reached the surface. Although a more sophisticated algorithm would be required to eliminate the false positives, encouraging data began to roll in.

I once again agreed to hit the financing trail, despite the hard lessons learned about attempting to diagnose and treat cancer. The "C" word spooked off two-thirds of our potential investors, and the others began asking tough questions that we should have expected. We were so caught up with the technology and our own story that we failed to do the proper homework.

A meeting with an FDA examiner was scheduled, and we soon learned that we'd have to complete an enormous study—more than a thousand patients with a complicated control group. The fundraising goal would need to be pushed into the double-digit million dollar range. We quickly reconsidered a dramatic "edit" of our story. Seeking FDA clearance as a "screening tool" rather than attempting to prove that we could eliminate a skin biopsy for early diagnosis would be a quick path to the market. Unfortunately, that story didn't hold water with the clinicians. The cost of a system, including a dedicated room in their practice, AND the continued cost of sending out the sample for pathology, no longer made this an enticing proposition. Another great story to diagnose and treat cancer would be locked away in a file cabinet because of exuberant costs and regulatory requirements... regardless of how we told the story of **SOLARIBUS**.

Story #8 – Development of an Implantable Autofocusing Lens

You want to do what... and put it where? I wasn't sold right away on the concept, but the degree of difficulty made it obvious that not many would attempt to even try to build the damn thing. *"I'm your guy,"* I heard myself say aloud once again. *Damn it!*

I met the founders of the 'parent company' at a Vision Expo in Boston—or was it New York? The meeting and how I got there was a blur as I literally watched a bench-top model of a large lens bring the print beneath it come into focus. It was a liquid crystal optic that changed power when activated with a small electrical current. They manually continued to turn the power on and off, focusing and defocusing the words below. The fundamentals of the technology was compared to those polarized windows that would filter the sunlight and darken at the flip of a switch.

The parent company was well down the development road to designing an electro-active pair of spectacles (glasses) that would manually or automatically switch the lenses into reading glasses (for near vision), and then back again to 20/20 distance viewing when the reader looked up from reading. They were searching for a start-up CEO who would miniaturize the technology and build an electro-active, foldable lens that would fit inside the eye and compete with the artificial lenses in the $4 billion cataract lens market. I was already committed before boarding that departing flight from Boston— or was it New York... still not sure.

Within days of negotiating my employment contract, I was sitting with a group of hand-picked consultants and advisors—who would later become priceless members of my management team—to break down the basic elements of this complex, exciting story. We needed to simplify the science, assess where the known and hidden risks might be, how and where we would execute the development plan, determine staffing needs, and of course, how much capital would be needed to hit that next 'inflexion point' that would mitigate specific risks and increase our valuation.

From past experiences, I knew this story wouldn't be acceptable if the final device didn't feel and look like a lens that ophthalmic surgeons were inserting every day throughout the world. Cataract surgery, to replace the aging, cloudy natural lens of a patient, is reported to be the most prevalent surgical procedure in the world, with over twenty million cases done each year. The final design had to use the existing insertion techniques, and be provided at a competitive price. The initial advantages were clear and an easy part of the story to tell... *"A conventional intraocular lens with the ability to manually or automatically autofocus from far to near... like the lens on your camera."*

We raised sufficient capital from the existing investors of the parent company—who'd already been hooked before I updated the story. Other investors were scarce. Despite the amazing story we had to tell, this was a pioneering effort to place microelectronics and rechargeable batteries "inside" the eye. Everyone wanted to continue to hear this exciting story, but didn't have the courage to come along for the journey.

We were forced to then consider the involvement of another large corporation who dominated the market, had an appreciation for our technology and could even help mitigate other future risks. Corporate audiences are tough! They take forever to get on board, and often demand special rights for the privilege of doing business with them. However, the right corporate partnership, at the right time, could add enormous credibility to your story.

Edit or move the goal post? Actually both. This corporate "partner" would lead the next round of financing if we agreed to abandon our current design and leap to a second generation design that had been part of our story to simply show our vision of how the technology should evolve. We'd agreed, but the story, timing, and amount of required capital all had to change. Our advanced audience made demands that we had to accept in order to stay on our journey.

Their view of inherent risks were different than other potential investors. They were not concerned about the micro-electronics or implantable power cells, they wanted proof we could develop an algorithm using a reliable physiological trigger that would activate the autofocusing power of the lens. The most viable "trigger" was the change in pupil size—which gets larger (dilates) when we look far, and smaller (constricts) when we look near. We agreed to co-sponsor a 350 patient study in which we would collect the appropriate data that could be used to design AND validate the algorithm residing on our proprietary microchip. A microscopic photo-sensor would be embedded in the lens to measure the movement of pupils and tell the system when to "turn on."

The story deepened as we determined that the data, algorithm and micro-processors provided us with three additional features; 1) the ability to make the system 'self-learning'—an artificial intelligence that would allow the system to adapt to the individual's specific pupil changes, 2) the ability to turn ON and OFF the system (focus far and near) by having the patient use a specific blink pattern, and 3) the ability for the physician to use a hand-held device to reprogram the system during the life of the patient. A radio-frequency (RF) microcoil was encapsulated within the peripheral edge of the lens for wireless recharging of the batteries (once each week for two hours while the patient was asleep).

This microcoil would also allow for an RF link for the reprogramming of the device, and would allow the system to send, receive and store data. It was a miniature pacemaker that resided inside the eye that would first be used for *autofocusing*, but eventually be the source to drive implantable drug delivery pumps and gating mechanism to sense and regulate intraocular pressure related to Glaucoma. Yes indeed... we had yet another damn tiger by the tail!

At first we thought it was another flying monkey, zooming in on us to disrupt our journey. Google Glass hit the front page of every tech magazine and newspaper business section. Google? Weren't they a search engine technology who just ventured into the cell phone business? I suppose it wasn't a far reach for them to get into 'wearable computing,' but the distraction was annoying. Our audience members were constantly asking how we compared to Google Glass. Well... first, our technology is an implant, not for gaming, navigating, taking pictures or recording videos... at least not yet. Secondly, our product is a medical device, regulated by the FDA and other international regulatory agencies. And finally, if such technology replicated Google Glass within an implantable device, it would cause such distraction and annoyance that laws would need to be passed to control it's use during driving, in classrooms, and during flights.

But, as previously mentioned in Chapter 14, we are often driven to edit our story according to the input of our audience. I pressed our Chief Technical Officer to explore what it would take to create a 'heads-up display' projected from our implanted lens. Would we have the capacity to upload/download programs to our implantable microchips? What would be required to capture an image and then send it to your iPhone? Okay... it was all possible, anything was possible, but more work and more money would be required.

To stay on our yellow brick road, and to be consistent with our mission, we decided to take our exploration one step further. Just ONE step. With the RF link technology we would be able to communicate with other implantable sensors under development by other med-tech companies. For example, one that would measure blood glucose levels in diabetic patients. These sensors were designed to send *real-time* data to an external reader... or even a smart phone. Why not use our lens as a means to collect such data and project it as a holographic digital display about one meter in front of our patient's eyes? By pixelating our lens, and using a secondary lens (perhaps a contact lens or even our own cornea), we would be able to create our own heads-up display. Oh... and how about a 4x zoom lens or the ability to take a photograph or photocopy from your implantable lens at the blink of an eye?

Well, I should stop here before this storyteller enters a deeper zone of embellishment. As of the publishing of this book, the company, **ELENZA**, is on the verge of identifying new investors, corporate partners and even potential military/DARPA grants. Yes, we are also exploring the capability of downloading facial recognition software onto this lens. Google Glass? Huh... bring it!

Story #9 – Another Eye Implant (A Special Project)

Many compelling stories for new ventures are generated out of personal need or from an experience touching one's family member. My brother, Randy, was severely myopic as a young boy. He'd worn thick glasses since pre-school and his distance vision only became worse with age. Lasik surgery wasn't an option. There wasn't enough cornea that could be cut and altered to provide any substantive correction to his vision.

At the age of fifty, he decided to try a new elective procedure that was starting to become more widely accepted. He would pay an ophthalmic surgeon to remove the natural lenses inside his eyes and replace them with artificial, acrylic lenses. This is the same procedure mentioned in the previous ELENZA story, except his natural lenses have not yet aged to the point of becoming *cataracts*. Insurance companies and Medicare reimburse costs associated with the replacement of cataract lenses, but the impaired vision needs to be well-diagnosed and documented by an Ophthalmologist. Therefore, he'd be forced to pay out of pocket for these new fancy lenses. And pay, he did!

His surgery went well, and within several weeks of his first incision he'd thrown away those thick Coke-bottle lenses. It was a life changing event. All was good… until the lights went out!

He and his wife were driving back from a trip in Minnesota to their home in Wisconsin when a black spot suddenly appeared in the center of one of his eyes. Like a bug resting on the television screen, it was annoying, and he focused on it while contemplating what it might be. Perhaps a floater in his eye? His doctor warned him of such a side-effect. But this was not moving, not floating. By the time he mustered the courage to tell his wife, it had tripled in size. Their drive and conversation continued as the spot continued to grow. His wife took over as the driver and headed directly to the closest hospital. Was it a brain tumor? They both feared the worst.

Good news, bad news... it wasn't his brain... but the retina in the back of his eye was fully detached. Patients suffering with severe myopia have a high incidence of retinal detachment and the surgical replacement of their lenses dramatically increases the possibility of detachment. His doctor may have ripped off the verbal list of potential complications, but "retinal detachment" didn't come to mind as that darkness spread rapidly across Randy's vision. But his problem had only begun—as is this story.

The two to three hour procedure to re-attach his retina, the thin layer of light-sensitive tissue in the back of the eye responsible for vision, was more complex than the 15-20 minute replacement of his lenses. The surgeon would evacuate the thick vitreous fluid from inside his eye with a cutting and suctioning device in order to obtain access to the detached retina. He'd then use a laser to flatten and tack the torn retina to the surrounding orbit of the eye. When completed, the eye would be filled with gas or silicone oil to temporarily replace the vitreous fluid to maintain appropriate pressure against the retina while it healed. The body would eventually replace the gas or oil with new vitreous fluids—over time. Meanwhile, the patient had to sleep and hold their head in a certain prone position in order for the gas/oil to maintain a constant pressure against the retina.

Three months following the retinal repair procedure, my brother was still complaining of poor vision, discomfort, headaches and the need to wear glasses once again. *Wait a minute... tell me about that procedure again? They sucked out the natural fluid and used a photocoagulation laser to burn the retina to the back of your eye? There's got to be a better way!*

Back in the early 90s, while at MICROVENA—the first story mentioned in this chapter—we developed a series of Nitinol, self-expanding stent-like devices. Had anyone thought about using this approach to "stent" or re-suspend the detached retina? A quick patent search didn't reveal anything that I had contemplated, so the essence of a new story started forming in my head. Sketches of several designs materialized on the back of a notebook. A literature search regarding the procedure, the physiology of the retina, related complications, historical solutions, failed cases, and the barbaric approach to a complex problem spurred me on. I was on to something... I was hooked once again.

As I reached for the phone to call my patent attorney, I told myself that I would not add more stress to my life by creating another company. Yeah, that's it... I would make this nothing more than a "project" —not a company. *Repeat after me... a project, not a company.* Yet the project needed to be protected, it needed a solid story behind it. Three weeks later an extensive patent application with nearly fifty claims were filed with the U.S. Patent Office.

The story took form as I drafted the provisional application for the attorney. My next call was to a local engineer who was recognized as the key developer of one of the most successful coronary stents marked by a division of Johnson & Johnson. Together we expanded the depth of the patent protection and enhanced the story, at this point, not for anyone except ourselves.

We didn't have an audience until we decided to solicit the advice of two local well-respected retinal surgeons. Rather than refer to this device as a "stent," a term not well-known to these eye surgeons, we decided it might be more descriptive to call it an "internal scaffold," one that would match the internal pressures of a normal eye. If inserted in such a way, we might possibly prove there would be no need to remove all the vitreous fluid of the eye, no need to burn the retina with a laser, and no need to fill the void with oil or gas. Vision should be restored in a fraction of the time, with less trauma, and reduced costs. When both of these audience members replied, *it should work, why hasn't anyone thought of this before...?*, we knew we were on to something! With the aid of LegalZoom.com, we formed a Limited Liability Corporation ("LLC") the next week and included the engineer and two surgeons as co-founders of our new little project.

The story turned into an Executive Summary and a brief PowerPoint presentation, necessary to pitch a local engineering firm to have them quote the construction of prototypes that we can test and validate on the bench. We ordered human cadaver eyes—yes, you'd be surprised what you can order over the internet—in order to learn more about the construction of the retina and to create a mold (a "caste") of the inside of the eye to ensure our design configuration was correct. We then met with the Biomedical Engineering Department at the Florida Institute of Technology to discuss their willingness to work with us on modeling the design and to simulate the functionality of the implanted scaffold. They were not only "willing," but eager. I had a research proposal from their administrators in my Inbox by the end of the week. We needed to raise some money. The costs were exceeding what my personal checking account would allow.

Telling the story to another lawyer friend of mine, he was not only immediately hooked, but he offered his services for a small piece of equity. Unfortunately, in preparation for a formal fundraising effort—no matter how large or small—he convinced me to convert the LLC to a Delaware C-Corporation which we would name **OptiSTENT**. *Damn it... I really didn't want to start another company! Here we go.*

The financing memorandum went out to a select group of private investors who I knew would "get the story" by simply reading my Executive Summary. One or two phone calls later, I had secured the financing needed to perform the modeling, simulation, prototype builds, and acute animal studies to provide "Proof of Science." Including patent prosecution costs, this little project would "live or die" by the quality of the animal data with total paid in capital of approximately $150,000. As of the publishing of this book, we are weeks away of learning whether we are going to tell a more detailed story to raise additional capital to pursue human clinical testing, or going back to the lab to iterate a more optimal design.

Story #10 – A Non-medical Venture

There are several other start-up stories to tell here, but I thought this non-medical venture might be of interest to those of you who have grown weary with reading about lab work, biology, chemistry, and the sacrifice of small furry animals for the betterment of mankind. This is also a classic re-start story, and an example of what might occur from the exuberance of aggressively pursuing something that *could* have just been a nice little hobby.

During the second season of volunteering as an assistant coach on my daughter's local softball team, I finally found the time to ask the head coach, Jack, what he did for a living. *If I'm not asked this question, then I don't ask it of others, for fear of the inevitable response of 'how about you... what do you do?' It's tough to explain that I'm just a storyteller without going into the lengthy details.*

Jack explained that he was a brewmaster at the local microbrewery—which I didn't even know existed. Shame on me, because I love beer, but shame on them for not providing sufficient marketing to make me a big consumer. Apparently, marketing was only part of the problem. Jack went on to vent his frustration over the existing management, not hiding the fact that he thought they were bumbling idiots. I actually looked for the beer, then under the labels of Indian River Brewery, but couldn't find it anywhere, and soon forgot about that gnawing thirst until I met Jack several months later, standing in line at the grocery store. He looked awful.

Holding up his hand, he stopped me mid-way through the story about my quest for his beer. "We're done," he said, "filing for bankruptcy... there's an auction this weekend if you're interested in any great brewing equipment... you can probably get it real cheap."

Okay, I know what you're thinking. *Just say no.* It actually kept me up all that night, wondering what it would take... wondering whether I had the credentials as a businessman and storyteller to get into brewing beer. Hey, it's 'fermentation chemistry' right? I have a background in biochemistry... close enough!

Yes, I went down to that broken-down brewery that Friday morning and pushed through the door to be greeted by the rancid smell of fermenting hops and barley. There was a thin, bald-headed guy, clipboard in hand, making his way through the large holding tanks and apparently struggling with how to value the bottling line stretched out in front of him.

I introduced myself and explained that Jack suggested I make an immediate visit. He barked back that he was the auctioneer, hired by the bankruptcy trustee, and that I was early.... "The auction is not until tomorrow."

Although the building appeared as if it were ready to collapse, the equipment was impressive looking. Large stainless steel fermentation silos stood in a long line, adjacent to them was the long sleek Italian-imported bottling line that included a pasteurization system, something only Coors was promoting at the time. The warehouse in the back was stacked to the ceiling with pallets full of cellophane-wrapped brown and green beer bottles waiting to be filled, six-pack carriers, collapsed cardboard boxes designed to hold full cases of beer, and endless rows of empty kegs. I had to ask my new bald-headed friend, "How much do you really think you'll get for all this and who the hell is going to buy a brewery in this small town?"

He shouldn't have told me, but without hesitation blurted out that they'd be lucky to find some sucker to buy the equipment for anything close to $120,000. The landlord was applying a great deal of pressure and the trustee managing the bankruptcy just didn't have enough time to advertise the auction outside of the local region. Something provided that *nudge* deep inside me and without thinking it through, I suggested that I'd buy everything for $75,000 and save them the time and expense of a formal auction. He glared back at me and explained that the equipment alone would cost nearly two million dollars to purchase as new. I shot back with, "... well it obviously ain't new!" Without taking his eyes from me, he dialed his cell phone, told someone on the other end about my offer, then said they would accept it IF I could bring them a certified bank check by the end of the business day. Done!

It was a long, painful weekend. Buyer's remorse set in quickly as I thought about the time, effort and energy that would be required to turn around a business I knew nothing about... AND, there was the other thing called my 'day job' that was already sucking up sixty hours each week. Jack! I had to have Jack on board with this.

By the time I phoned him, he'd already heard about his new owner and I sensed a bit of both happiness and sarcasm in his voice on the other end of the line. I cancelled my day-job meetings for Monday and asked him to call together the employees for a meeting at the brewery... *with their new owner*. As I recall, there were now only six remaining workers, including Jack, the brewmaster, and the head of marketing who Jack suggested that I make President of the brewery. He seemed to understand general operations and bookkeeping and had a way of schmoozing—another form of storytelling—which was needed to reel in the landlord who was waiting on eviction notices. My desperation for needing a day-to-day operating guy overweighed my concerns of his marketing skills. I still wondered why I never knew there was a microbrewery in my backyard, but convinced myself that I could add value to that element of the story.

I actually didn't have much of a *story* to tell those employees in those initial days, except that there was a new sheriff in town and that the brewery was "under new management." That and a few personal checks to pay off the angry vendors—including that landlord—seemed to buy us some time. It was too early to think about crafting a story for new investors, so we focused on coming up with a story for the Press Release to help establish a new image for the brewery. It was the first step in an exhaustive new marketing plan that had to be put into place. I quickly learned about the two new essential components to this particular story: distribution and marketing.

The products were good. Jack was actually an accomplished brewer with formal college training in the art, and an apprenticeship in Germany where he picked up some trade-secrets of his own. We'd deal with the name of the brewery later, but the immediate focus needed to be in the consolidation and re-labeling of the beers. The labels were old and despite several years of prior efforts, still had no brand recognition.

While working on new product names and labels, we also took the chance on another opportunity to license a well-established Irish Hard Cider. This was a product that was selling well in Ireland, called *Kelley's Traditional Hard Cider*, and we were provided the exclusive option to license and produce the product for all of N. America. It required an upfront fee, small royalty on the net sales of the product, and a commitment to exclusively purchase the thick, fermenting base that was made from traditional cider apples grown in Ireland. This cider base would fill a freight car and be shipped by boat to the U.S., then mixed with one of our light beers using a secret recipe. The result was a high-alcohol, beer-based, clear, crisp hard cider. Although we needed—and obtained—a wine license to produce it, we marketed this as a malt beverage that came in a classic beer bottle, yet tasting like a sweet, alcohol-rich apple cider. I included the use of the name in the license for the cider base. The female market loved it and our little brewery was soon 'back on the map.'

As our President was working on distribution throughout the State of Florida and contracts with large grocery store chains, I focused on expanding the business. Another brewery named after its location, Ybor City, was owned and operated by a third generation brewer from South America. They'd also run into financial problems and wanted me to consider "contract manufacturing" their beers, while they also focused on sales and marketing. At first our small team viewed this as 'enabling a competitor,' but we desperately needed to expand our volume to obtain some operating efficiencies. We eventually worked out the terms of a contract and purchased all of their equipment and started to retro-fit it into our existing facility. The roof was leaking, the warehouse was now probably a fire-hazard, and I was having more equipment shipped from the Tampa area. My team thought I was out of my mind.

Ironically, months later, my South American friend called to say he could no longer make the payment on the last two shipments of bottled and kegged beer. Sales were suffering— probably due to our renewed presence in the market—and he'd decided to move back to Argentina where his family was running one of the largest breweries in the continent. We negotiated a settlement on what was owed and took possession of his labels. Unfortunately, I was also running out of my own cash reserves and I needed a partner. Time to draft a strong story and look for an appropriately deep-pocketed audience who might have the thirst for the craft brewing industry.

A little bit of luck actually comes your way once in a while. I identified a half-dozen high net worth individuals in the local area whom I'd target with my new story. We needed just one to join me on this journey, and indeed just *one* showed any interest. Ed was a wealthy individual who was pouring money into the community, and just opened up a world-class Tennis Club in town. His wife was already a fan of our Hard Cider and our discussions acceler-ated. The only hitch was that he wanted to invest enough capital to have a controlling interest; 51%

ownership. I'd agree, as long as I had the ability to set the valuation of the business, to ensure that we'd have enough working capital to grow. We signed the deal within thirty days.

As a co-founder and minority shareholder, I once again found myself along for the ride—on someone else's journey. The ambition of this wealthy partner of mine didn't stop there. We went on to acquire the assets of both The Key West Brewery and the Miami Brewing Company. As you can imagine, my position was further diluted with all the acquisitions and follow-on financings. My total investment of $775,000 was dwarfed by the millions needed to build what is now known as the **Florida Beer Company**. The brewery has won multiple Gold Medals in brewing contests throughout the U.S. and is now ranked as one of the larger regional breweries in the country. Yes... they let me stop by anytime to pick up a case or two for the weekend.

BONUS Story – Becoming a Novelist

During the editing of the manuscript for this book, I was encouraged to consider one more story for this chapter. It was already nice and tidy, exactly ten stories, all of nearly equal length, all designed to provide appropriate examples of the importance of *storytelling* in being a true entrepreneur. After revisiting many of the interviews and guest blogs I've done over the past couple of years to promote my novels, I came to realize that those voices of encouragement were absolutely correct... being a published author requires the same elements of *storytelling* that is necessary for being an entrepreneur. In fact, I've already gone on record by stating my belief that publishing a novel today requires a great deal of entrepreneurship. Therefore, I hope this final story encourages each and every one of you to step out and try your hand at getting your own novel published. You can do it!

As stated above, there are plenty of websites where I have been interviewed about what stimulated me to start writing novels. Without a doubt, there was a specific *spark*—that concept of a story that swirled in my head for over a decade—then eventually that *nudge*—during an extended cruise with my wife, with what seemed like endless time on my hands. She encouraged me—actually dared me—to start writing that first manuscript. Little did I know then, how similar this journey would become to those told previously in this chapter. However, there was added complexity to the risks, costs, time and energy required to write and publish a novel. The obvious audience was the potential unknown mass of readers of my proposed 'thrillers.' What I didn't contemplate was that, in order to get my work published, I needed to address an entirely different intermediate audience, one that included literary agents, publishers, editors and publicists.

The first manuscript was originally called *Harvest of the Unborn*... a very bold, scary medical thriller based on true events... untold secrets of what I'd experienced as a pre-med student involving genetic research using aborted fetuses. It took over a year to draft and revise, forcing me to revisit and analyze many segments of my personal and professional life which would be crafted into fictional scenes. It was therapeutic and exciting.

With a finished manuscript (the product) in hand, I found myself considering how best to tell the story... and to whom. I knew nothing about the publishing industry, but had read enough about e-books—electronic publishing—and self-publishing to know what questions I needed to ask. I turned to an old colleague whom I'd remembered was a published author, one of his many interesting side-jobs. Gerry had also just completed a 'how-to' book called *Magic for Your Writing: Help for the*

Aspiring Writer. Perfect timing! He soon became my first audience member.

As it turned out, Gerry was also spending a good portion of his time professionally editing manuscripts for a select number of new authors. He was eager to take on one more project and we spent the next six months *repairing* what I thought was already a finished story. This could have been referred to as *editing,* but since I had no real formal training in literature, or the skill of writing, Gerry had to teach me the fundaments of writing fiction. I tried skimming his book along the way, but I figured it was better to get it directly from the master's own mouth. It was painful, but it forced me to understand and appreciate proper grammar, sentence structure, and different characters' points of view.

After beating that manuscript into shape, he then convinced me to avoid self-publishing. The decision complemented my ego and desire to go 'old-school'... to actually search and find a world-class literary agent and a publisher. I had visions of seeing *Harvest of the Unborn* in the windows of every bookstore and on the stands of every airport shop that I'd pass multiple times a week during my travels. I'd quickly learn, however, that this was just another *trough of disillusionment* often experienced by all of us entrepreneurs!

My story was captured in the form of a query letter sent out to over sixty different literary agents and publishers. The onslaught of rejection letters reminded me of those received in response to my applications to medical schools several decades ago. As a first-time author, I had no brand recognition and was pitching a story called *Harvest of the Unborn*, about the pirating of organs from aborted fetuses. More research on my audience was required, and I soon identified three top literary agents in Manhattan who had represented similar 'edgy' novels. I honed in on one in particular and pursued them just as I had previously fished for the best venture capitalist to join me in my other journeys.

I was in New York for other business and had my targeted agent's name already locked into my address book on my new Blackberry. I'd convinced myself that if I could just have a one-on-one meeting with this advanced-audience member that I could set the hook and reel her in. On the other end of the phone, her assistant indicated she'd see me "the next time I would be in New York." They were caught by surprise when I said I was mere blocks away, so they reluctantly agreed to see me... for fifteen minutes.

It wasn't long before I was sitting in front of Erica, telling my tale... presenting my bait. Once I got through the details surrounding the delicate issues of aborted fetuses, the story deepened with elements of human trafficking, the romance between two main characters, motives behind the evil-doers, and the eventual illicit black market for human organ transplants. As I approached the end of my tale, she inched forward in her chair and asked... "And then what?" I knew I had set the hook, but my naivety allowed me to believe that I was reeling her in.

Although they were no longer considering contracts with first-time authors (at the time), she was willing to consider representing me IF, and only if, one of their top independent editors would agree to work with me on the manuscript. What? I just spent six months editing and re-editing! You've got to be kidding me.

I had provided her with my *needs*; a contract with a well-respected literary agent, a publisher, and the support to build brand recognition. She then, in turn, provided me with her *ask* in return; to consider a professional edit with someone they knew and trusted. Once again, it was hard to say 'no.' Fortunately, one of their top editors voiced a strong interest to work with me on the manuscript and the second leg of my journey began.

Several months later, with a final-final manuscript in hand, my *agent* started to solicit the large publishing houses, but was running into another challenge... more of those damn flying monkeys. No one would touch the story with such a title from an unknown author. We not only needed to come up with a new title, but she'd asked me to find a prominent business person/author/physician who could provide me with a 'blurb' regarding my story for the front cover. I felt like I'd just tripped over another log on my journalistic yellow brick road.

Tenacity and persistence prevailed, and we finally had agreement on a new title, **EQUITY** *of* **EVIL**, and through a connection of a connection, I was waiting on a review from one of the most renowned, best-selling medical thriller authors, Dr. Robin Cook. The final elements of my story came together and the hook was taken by a publishing house that launched the eBook version in March of 2012 and a print version nearly six month later! I've since then been fine-tuning my story in promoting this novel to whomever would listen. This adventure also taught me about a new larger audience... those millions of potential audience members on the internet, accessible by something now known to me as 'social media.'

EQUITY of EVIL has gone on to receive four literary awards and has been recognized as one of the top medical thrillers on Amazon.com based on average customer reviews. Book two of this series, now known as The EQUITY Series, has been released under the title, *EQUITY of FEAR*. To my amazement, this series has been compared to Stieg Larsson's series, *The Girl with the Dragon Tattoo*. Yes, I would love to see this story play out on the big screen!

CHAPTER 20

The Author - Biography

WELL, YOU'D THINK THIS WOULD BE THE EASIEST STORY TO tell. However, I'm not sure how much more babbling about myself this audience would be interested in. You've already gotten to know my history pretty well in the analogies that I've used to tell my *Storytelling* story. But this may serve as a little additional insight as to *how* and *when* I may have learned these skills along the way. The road was a bit treacherous, but I think my expectations were low... at least in the early going. Those mentioned in the Acknowledgement of this book were kind enough to push, encourage, and often times, *throw* me back on to that yellow brick road.

IN THE BEGINNING (aka Once Upon a Time)

My father's family was from Naples, Italy and my mother from Vienna, Austria. An interesting mix, part Hungarian gypsy, part Italian American 'dago'... I was born to tell stories... and yes, I use my hands a lot when doing so. The only interesting part of this story is that they met in a bowling alley in Pittsburgh, the rest, as they say... was history.

Dad owned and operated a series of donut shops, where not only the dough was raised there, but two young boys; my brother and I. We were the classic "latchkey" kids, getting ourselves off to school in the morning and returning to an empty house—mom and dad worked 24/7 at the shop. When we were old enough, they had the bus drop us off not at home, but at the corner next to the shop. We didn't call it child labor back then, but we were paid just ten cents a day to flip donuts frying in the hot grease and to scrape the pans that collected the drippings from the glaze coatings. *Back then, ten cents would buy ya a donut and an endless cup of coffee.*

Somewhere along the line, my affinity for animals grew. I then got the notion that I wanted to be a veterinarian someday. I read what I could from our cherished set of Encyclopedia Britannica, which explained the importance of proper academic training. In speaking with our local vet, I then learned how difficult it was to get accepted to a school of Veterinarian Medicine—which was even more difficult than regular medical school. I stepped up my studies and saw it as the only way to avoid a life of filing cream donuts in Western Pennsylvania.

ACADEMICS

God does indeed work in mysterious ways. By the time I found my focus and entered junior high school, I was pleasantly *husky,* as my mom use to say. I preferred *husky* over "Donut Boy" —which was probably more accurate AND more appropriate. Even though we had one of those cement ponds ('swimming pools') in the backyard, there was no denying the effects of consuming donuts two to three times a day for over ten years. There may have been an attractive young man underneath all those folds, but the girls never saw it. I had very little distractions. Working at a nearby kennel, I shoveled dog crap twice a day, and spent the rest of my time studying or trying to swim some of that blubber off in the pool late into the evening.

By the time I started high school, I was leaned out enough to squeeze into a Speedo to try out for the varsity swim team. To my chagrin, I made the team and a year later I was both accepting a certificate for making the National Honor Society and sporting a smaller Speedo leading off our record-breaking relay team. Time flew by and both the demands of the team and advanced science classes kept me from experimenting with alcohol and a variety of recreational drugs that were as readily available then as energy drinks are today. I graduated from high school in 1976 at seventeen and started my pre-med studies that fall at the University of Pittsburgh.

Two part-time jobs were required to cover the expense of rent, tuition, books and food. There was not much time left for *organized* college sports such as swimming or water polo (which were both attempted), so I fed my need for athletics by signing up for the city's rugby team—the famed Pittsburgh Harlequin Rugby Club. HERE is where I first groomed my storytelling abilities. You see, to play on the city club, you had to be twenty-one years of age. In fact, I was recruited at a local bar, thanks to the assistance and altered drivers' license of my twenty-five year old roommate. I spent the next four years convincing my teammates, coaches, sponsors, and local bartenders that I was of legal age. Here I also learned and earned the right to define the terms; exaggerating, embellishing, and bullshitting.

I seemed to have also made the cut while my professors weeded out the massive pre-med students who were there for the wrong reasons. I kept my head down and studied hard—with an emphasis on biochemistry and cytology. Unfortunately, it became apparent that my grades weren't quite good enough for veterinarian school, but might be adequate for medical school. Finally completing my classes, I scrapped through the MCAT exams and sent out as many applications as I could afford while considering a combined MD/PhD program at a handful of institutions... not sure if I wanted to actually *practice* the Art of Medicine.

Rejections were painful, but I was finally placed on a waiting list at a Pennsylvania medical school. Waiting list? That was a kind way of saying that I was probably right at the bottom of the list and they were waiting to see if anyone better applied. I therefore jumped on an acceptance letter to attend a graduate program at UCLA—where I applied simply because I'd heard the local Santa Monica rugby team was one of the best in the country. Books and rugby boots in hand, I took a bus from Pittsburgh to Los Angeles where I would eventually abuse both my mind and body.

ACADEMIA to INDUSTRY

Due to what was referred to as Reaganomics back then, my graduate program was shifted from department to department until I finally settled in at the Department of Mathematical Sciences where I took course work in biophysics, genetic engineering and electron microscopy. Again, to pay the bills, I worked part time in the human genetics engineering laboratory on a grant-funded project to study 'ultra-structural cellular modifications relating to inherited metabolic diseases.' The only relevance here is that it allowed me to flex my creative muscles and work on the design of an implantable enzyme bioreactor to treat a variety of these disorders. It sparked my entrepreneurial spirit, taught me how to construct a story that tied together clinical problems and technology solutions, *and* the definition of intellectual property.

After eighteen months of sacrificing hundreds of lab rats, I started smelling like one—questioning how my early ambitions of becoming a veterinarian drove me from shoveling dog shit at the age of twelve to bagging rat shit at the age of twenty-two. Then an opportunity presented itself... one that could possibly be considered a *nudge*. I was asked to consider joining a medical device company in Indiana to help create a new division in the field of critical care medicine.

There was no turning back and my professional status as a "Storyteller" was just truly beginning.

EXECUTIVE MANAGEMENT

COOK Critical Care (Bloomington, IN)
– Director/Manager   1983 – 1989
MICROVENA, Inc. (St. Paul, MN)
– Founding-CEO   1989 – 1998
Image-guided NEUROLOGICS, (Melbourne, FL)
– Co-Founder/CEO   1998 – 2005
Accuitive Medical Ventures, (Duluth, GA)
– Managing Director   2005 – 2008
NovaVision, (Boca Raton, FL)
- Interim-CEO   2008 – 2010
ELENZA, Inc. (Roanoke, VA)
- President/CEO   2010 –

BOARD of DIRECTORS

MICROVENA (St. Paul, MN)   1983 - 1989
MicroPure Medical, Inc. (St. Paul, MN)   1993 - 1998
Vascular Science (Minneapolis, MN)   1996 - 1999
CytoGenesis, Inc. (Athens, GA)
– Chairman   1999 - 2005
Triton BioSystems, Inc. (Lawrence, MA)
– Chairman   1999 - 2006
TGS Innovations, Inc. (Bloomington, MN) 2008 – 2012
Q-Sensei, Inc. (Erfurt, Germany)
– Chairman   1999 –
NexGen Medical Systems, Inc. (Reno, NV) 2009 –
PingMD (New York, NY)   2010 –

ELENZA (Roanoke, VA)   2010 –
OptiSTENT, Inc. (Rockledge, FL)   2010 –
Greatbatch (Frisco, TX)   2012 –

EXITS

Vascular Science
    Acquired by St. Jude Medical   1999
MICROVENA
    Acquired by Warburg Pincus   2000
CytoGenesis
    Merger with BresaGen Ltd.   2001
Thermonix
    Merger with Triton BioSystems   2002
Image-Guided NEUROLOGICS
    Acquired by Medtronic, Inc.   2004

HONORS and AWARDS

Who's Who Among Rising Young Americans
    - Business Citation Awards   1991, 1992, 1993
The Rolex Enterprise Award of Excellence   1993
Who's Who in International Business
    - Citation Award   1994
Who's Who in Executives & Businesses   1997
Minnesota's Technology Leadership Award 1997
    - Sponsored by 3M, Honeywell & Medtronic
Who's Who in Executives & Businesses   1998
Honorary Chairman of the Congressional   2003 – 2005
Business Advisory Council

Ernst & Young Entrepreneur of the Year Award 2004
- Presented by Ernst & Young
Businessman of the Year   2005
- Presented by the National Congressional Committee
Entrepreneur of the Year Award   2013
- Presented by the Business Intelligence Group

AWARD-WINNING AUTHOR (Fiction)

EQUITY of EVIL – Book ONE of The EQUITY Series (Released March 2012)
    ISBN: 978-1-60619-236-8; Publisher: Twilight Times Books (eBook Version)
    ISBN: 978-1-60619-237-5; Publisher: Paladin Timeless Books (Print Version)

EQUITY of FEAR – Book TWO of The EQUITY Series (Released March 2013)
    ISBN: 978-1-60619-248-1; Publisher: Twilight Times Books (eBook Version)
    ISBN: 978-1-60619-249-8; Publisher: Paladin Timeless Books (Print Version)

CHAPTER 21

The Nuggets – In Case You Forgot

ISUPPOSE YOU CAN VIEW THIS AS THE CRIB NOTES TO THIS book, those little nuggets that someone like Sarah Palin might have scribbled on the inside of her hand. They're not critical, but something that summarizes the key elements of this particular story. I sincerely hope you find them of some value, and look forward to reading, hearing or learning of your own fascinating story someday!

◆

Be true to yourself. You're the only one who really knows what's right for your mind and soul, and the relationship you have with your family. Don't bend to external pressures to compromise who you really are. Don't fall victim to the Peter Principle... it will certainly lead to failure.

◆

Proper storytelling requires some basic elements: understanding who your audience is, what they specifically might be interested in hearing, and determining the best way to "hook" and "fight" them through the process of reeling, giving them line, preventing them from getting snagged, and... in other words, keeping their interest sufficient to stimulate moving them forward to the next deeper phase of your story.

◆

Your story needs to evolve and mature as you and your audience do. Watch how they respond, listen to their comments and suggestions. Allow them to help you fine-tune your story.

◆

Before even telling your story for the first time, think it through, lay out the key components, structure it properly and then rehearse, rehearse, rehearse.

◆

The written form of your story—either the Executive Summary or PowerPoint Presentation—becomes the outline of the supportive materials that you'll need to provide in order to move to the next phase of your storytelling.

◆

Hone your storytelling skills whenever possible on less critical audiences. Build your confidence, style and flow of the story until it becomes natural and comfortable.

◆

Construct your story to address as many anticipated elements as you believe your special audience will be looking for... and then some!

♦

Always return to the basic, fundamental elements when preaching to the choir. Reinforce those enticing features of your bait that originally hooked them. Praise your audience for their courage to join you, thank them for their dedication, and share the tidbits of good news along the way.

♦

Never bullshit or exaggerate. It's okay to pepper your story with a bit of embellishment, but do so with caution... and only after you have your audience hooked with the basic facts. It also is worth the time and costs to have professional legal review of any formal documents that you plan to put out on the street.

♦

Deflect the urge to provide that Elevator Speech before knowing more about your audience and having the proper time to set that hook in preparation for the tough fight to pull them on board.

♦

When editing or revising your story, only edit with a purpose. Think it through and make sure your story maintains the continuity of your previously told stories for the purpose of achieving specific objectives.

◆

Reinventing your company requires a bold new story. It's often beneficial to commit to reinventing the company before there's even a recognizable need. It doesn't come naturally and takes a great deal of courage.

◆

Successful storytellers (and entrepreneurs) should realize that there will be times when they'll need to get off the path, to deviate, take a shortcut which turns out not to be necessarily shorter, but perhaps more appropriate to ensure that you'll get to your final destination. It's important to anticipate this in your journey... for many of us who tend to wander, this is inevitable. We may even get lost in the woods at times, but when it happens, just collect yourself, find a point of direction, listen for appropriate signals, and work your way back to that yellow brick road. The alternative of letting go of your story or loss of desire to get back on that road could be devastating.

◆

For advanced audiences, you'll need support and processes in place to continue telling your story, and to ensure it is told properly. Start with partnering with the Chairman of your Board. I personally think it is wise to keep the CEO and Chairman roles separated so that you broaden the team who is responsible for messaging and communication with your growing audience. Challenge your Chairman to build a consensus regarding Board-related matters. Keep your Directors engaged and make sure there's a succession plan in place to assist with replacing those who are not... and sooner if you sense any insanity.

♦

In today's economic environment and new slog of investors, focused on getting in on the next social media fad or mobile app for a quick return on their investment, its critical to map out your exit strategy sooner than later. However, be cautious and deliberate when constructing an alternative ending to your story... you may only have one or two chances to do so. In doing so too often, you'll appear careless, even reckless... stepping off the yellow brick road looking for cover... and dodging flying monkeys!

♦

Strive to perfect the Art of Storytelling. Once you do, be sure to mentor and help others to continue the art. Start with your key employees. Join the Boards of other companies and become engaged with their messaging and communication of their vision and corporate mission. Hold on to the Art.

◆

Stay on that yellow brick road!